CULTURAL COMPETENCY HANDBOOK

Volume I
Practical Strategies for Classroom Instruction

Edited by Timothy Forde

NEW FORUMS

NEW FORUMS PRESS INC.

Published in the United States of America
by New Forums Press, Inc.1018 S. Lewis St.
Stillwater, OK 74074
www.newforums.com

Copyright © 2018 by New Forums Press, Inc.

All rights reserved. No part of this publication may be reproduced or transmitted in any form or by any means, electronic or mechanical, including photocopy, or any information storage or retrieval system, without permission in writing from the publisher.

Library of Congress Cataloging-in-Publication Data Pending

This book may be ordered in bulk quantities at discount from New Forums Press, Inc., P.O. Box 876, Stillwater, OK 74076 [Federal I.D. No. 73 1123239]. Printed in the United States of America.

ISBN 10: 1-58107-314-3
ISBN 13: 978-1-58107-314-0

Contents

Introduction v
  Timothy Forde
1. The Limits of Evidence..1
  DeDe Wohlfarth, Truman Harris, & Jimmy Joseph
2. Understanding the Impact of and Addressing Classroom Microaggressions..21
  RoShunna Lea, Catherine Burke, Adriana Peña, Jimmy Joseph, & DeDe Wohlfarth
3. Cultural Competency: An Organizing Principle for Effective Partnerships Between Academic and Student Affairs..37
  Natalie Gibson
4. Multicultural Relationships within the Academic Setting: The Influence of Power and Cultural Trust 49
  Adriana Peña, Roshunna Lea, Catherine Burke, Virginia Frazier, & DeDe Wohlfarth
5. Bridging the Digital Divide by Decreasing the Power Differential in Online and Hybrid Classrooms................65
  Michael Daniel, Mackenzie Hoffman, & DeDe Wohlfarth
6. Black Men in Higher Education 79
  Steven Kniffley, Truman Harris, Jimmy Joseph, & DeDe Wohlfarth
7. Allowing for a Silent Pause: Introverts in Higher Education..97
  Meena Kumar, Nisha Kumar, & DeDe Wohlfarth
8. Trigger Warnings in the Classroom 113
  Catherine Burke, Kaitlyn Hoitomt, Carson Haynes, & DeDe Wolhfarth
9. Responding to Gender and Sexual Identity Diversity in the College Classroom 127
  Tara Tuttle
About the Authors..147

Introduction

By Timothy Forde

Today's classrooms are increasing in number of students from ethnically, culturally and linguistically diverse backgrounds. Despite all of reform efforts on teacher education there remains a gap in academic achievement between White students and minority students. There is some evidence that teachers who are culturally competent are successful in improving the academic achievement of minority students.

As citizens we have an obligation and duty to redress the persistent achievement gaps that exist due to the changing demographics including the facts that more school age children speak a language other than English at home, immigrants represent a growing number of students in the classroom and disproportionate numbers of minority students are referred to special education classes. Given the prior democratic imperatives, the book is an initial attempt to provide educators with strategies, resources and activities that can be used to develop culturally competence.

Our first goal is not to learn more about the complexity of student backgrounds' although this is a necessary first step, but rather to help teachers become reflective critical thinkers about their own cultural identities, experiences and biases so they can begin to develop thoughtful, tranformative, instructional practices in the classroom so that all students can have a successful academic career. Educators have a moral obligation to educate all our students to function effectively in our pluralistic democratic society. Our second goal is to help students develop the knowledge, attitudes and skills needed to participate in their cultural communities as effective, emphatic and thoughtful citizens. To help students achieve these goals, the culture of the classroom and the curriculum must be substantially reframed and educators must acquire new knowledge, attitude and skills.

This book, *Cultural Competency: A Handbook for Educators, Volume I,* is designed primarily to help higher education instructors identify and clarify the philosophical and definitional issues related to cultural competency, understand and appreciate multiple perspectives and ways of knowing, and provide strategies and recommendations for inclusive teaching and learning practices for faculty who are designing curriculum. Additionally, many chapters include instructional strategies that can be used in the classroom. This first volume consists of nine chapters which are briefly described below.

Chapter 1 The Limits of Evidence

This chapter highlights six themes from the SoTL (Scholarship of Teaching and Learning) literature that help bridge the gap between evidence based best teaching and culturally responsive teaching.

Chapter 2 Understanding the Impact of and Addressing Classroom Microaggressions

This chapter provide a brief overview of the literature on microaggressions, discusses how microaggressions commonly transpire in college classrooms, and provides strategies to effectively address microaggressions.

Chapter 3 Cultural Competency: An Organizing Principle For Effective Partnerships Between Academic And Student Affairs

This chapter will explore the use of cultural competency as a guiding principle for developing effective partnerships between student and academic affairs in the community college setting.

Chapter 4 Multicultural Relationships within the Academic Setting: The Influence of Power and Cultural Trust

This chapter discusses strategies that can be used to create an academic environment that fosters inclusivity and decreases animosity between different racial, cultural, and ethnic members of the academic community.

Chapter 5 Bridging the Digital Divide by Decreasing the Power Differential in Online and Hybrid Classrooms

This chapter will explore the challenges students of color face when they enroll in online courses. The authors will offer recommendations that professors can use to improve the academic achievement students of color.

Chapter 6 Black Men in Education

Key barriers to Black male education include generationally transmitted learned helplessness in educational settings, false attributions of a racialized masculinity, and ineffective peer leadership. This chapter will explore these barriers using the contextual and developmental narrative of a Black male named Brandon.

Chapter 7 Allowing for a Silent Pause: Introverts in Higher Education

This chapter discusses research regarding introversion in the classroom and suggests practical suggestions for professors to better meet the learning needs of introverted students.

Chapter 8 Trigger warnings in the classroom

This chapter will review research on how college students' past experiences with the law may inform cultural identities, impact classroom performance and engagement, and impair future employment success.

Chapter 9 Responding to Gender and Sexual Identity Diversity in the College Classroom

This chapter will discuss how to reconceptualize the college classroom in ways that better serve LGBTQIA students. The author offers several strategies that can be used in the classroom to ensure that all students experience a sense of belonging in the classroom.

Chapter One

The Limits of Evidence

By DeDe Wohlfarth, Truman Harris, & Jimmy Joseph

This chapter highlights six themes from the SoTL (Scholarship of Teaching and Learning) literature that help bridge the gap between evidence based best teaching and culturally responsive teaching. The themes addressed include: power differentials, imposter syndrome, conversations of race, cross-cultural relationships, supporting the "only," and cultural humility. As key articles are discussed in each area, we also share practical recommendations for professors to create culturally competent learning environments.

This chapter provides practical solutions to creating culturally inclusive classrooms that welcome all students. Creating collaborative classrooms begins with professors, as we set the tone in the classroom. It also requires multiple strategies, including: 1) reducing the power differential between professors and students; 2) actively challenging the imposter syndrome; 3) facilitating meaningful yet difficult conversations about race; 4) building authentic cross-cultural relationships; 5) supporting students as "the only;" and 6) practicing cultural humility.

Author Introductions

Before tackling these topics, we would like to introduce ourselves as the co-authors of the chapter. Our names are DeDe Wohlfarth, Truman Harris, and Jimmy Joseph. We are one white female professor of psychology and two Black male doctoral students of psychology. Our demographics influence our perspectives, and we want to be honest about ourselves. Jimmy is a Haitian Black man who loves fried goat, is originally from West Palm Beach, Florida, and finds solace in writing and being involved in long, respectful conversations on differing opinions. Truman is a Black man who enjoys exercise and weight-lifting, is a strong political activist for human rights and environmental and economic justice, and has lived in both rural and urban areas of Kentucky. DeDe is White female who lives in a 100-year-old farmhouse, loves running and sushi, and has four teenagers who daily expand her sense of humor.

Those brief snapshots share only surface-level information about who we are, but ironically, you now know more about us than you do about most academic authors. We are deliberately introducing ourselves so we can begin to uncover the assumptions of whiteness that pervade many of our scientific and academic endeavors, masquerading as the cloak of objectivity and rational empiricism. Our gender, race, culture and age affect our worldview and thus how we write this chapter. To be clear, we are not against objectivity and empiricism, and highly value research and evidence. However, we are daily challenged by the limitations of evidence, which serves as the segue for this chapter's rationale.

The Back Story to this Chapter

We were inspired to write this essay because of a research quest. Specifically, we wanted to know if the Scholarship of Teaching Learning (SoTL) literature supported a syllabus containing specific welcome statements for students of color. We believed that such statements would help decrease the power differential between professors and students, encourage students to challenge existing paradigms, and increase student motivation and engagement. Finding no research to support our hypothesis, we decided to conduct our own. In the process, we grew disenchanted with the existing SoTL research. The problem is that research, by definition, can only look backwards. It analyzes data that has already been gathered and events that already happened. Thus, the SoTL research predominantly focuses on the students who have been represented in many classrooms (predominately White, middle or upper socio-economic status students, and increasingly female) but not the students who have been missing from our classrooms (predominantly students of color, and/or lower socio-economic students, and especially males of color).

As a practical example of the limitations of research, consider our discipline of psychology. Currently, African American psychologists account for 5% of the practicing workforce, and only 30% of these individuals are male. These percentages have been stagnant for almost a decade. Nationwide, African American males are one of the most underrepresented groups in the field of Psychology (Lin, Nigrinis, Christidis & Stamm, 2015). So, when our field conducts research on multicultural competence, although focused on people of color, it is primarily conducted with and by white individuals. By extrapolation: How can we create classrooms for the students of tomorrow when our research reflects the students of yesterday? In some situations, do we, as a group of experts, have a moral obligation to transcend the limits of research by making recommendations that are not yet research supported, or is this a dangerous precedent?

Chapter Objectives

This chapter will highlight a few themes from the SoTL literature that help bridge the gap between evidence based best teaching and culturally responsive teaching. The chapter specifically focuses on six themes: power differential, imposter syndrome, conversations of race, cross-cultural relationships, supporting the "only," and cultural humility. We will also share practical recommendations to create *culturally competent learning environments.*

Six Research-Supported Pedagogical Practices to Create Culturally Competent Learning Environments

1. Reducing the Power Differential between Professors and Students

Learner-Centered Teaching is a philosophical approach to teaching that places student learning as the highest priority of all outcomes (Weimer, 2013). It challenges professors to move away from superficially "covering" course material through lecture-based classes. Instead, professors are encouraged to actively engage students in the hard, messy work of learning. This is done by motivating and empowering students. Learner-centered classrooms are collaborative and focus on student skill development, especially skills that are relevant to students' daily lives and eventual careers (Weimer, 2013).

Research supports adopting a learner-centered approach. In a summary of multiple studies on teacher-centered (lecture style) vs. learner-centered (active learning) approaches, Trigwell (2010) noted that the teacher-centered style is associated with surface learning that is quickly forgotten by students. Learner-centered teaching is strongly and positively associated with deep learning because of its emphasis on getting students actively engaged in the material through self-directed learning, discussion and debates, and problem-based learning.

Learner-centered teaching encourages students to be self-directed learners who oversee the learning process, thereby increasing their sense of control. In fact, even a syllabus written using learner-centered language inspires students. Richmond, Slattery, Mitchell, Morgan, and Becknell (2016) found that students rated learner-centered syllabi as more positive than traditional syllabi. Despite not having met the professor, students rated the professors who authored learner-centered syllabi as more creative, caring, happy, receptive, reliable and enthusiastic. More importantly, students expected to be more engaged in a learner-centered class—a critical variable as student engagement is highly correlated with student motivation and learning (Richmond, Slattery, Mitchell, Morgan & Becknell, 2016).

A key tenant of learner-centered teaching is to reduce the power differential between professors and students, to the extent that this is possible (Weimer, 2013). Although the reality is that professors retain the power of administering grades, it is students, ironically, and who have the ultimate power in a class. They can make teaching useless by simply refusing to learn. Decreasing the power differential between professors and students is particularly critical to students of color. The most current data available suggests that 78% of university professors in the United States are White (Kena, Hussar, McFarland, de Brey, Musu-Gillette, Wang, & Barmer, 2016). These individuals, including myself (Wohlfarth), have benefitted from the myriad of benefits granted by white privilege. Although White professors vary greatly in their own educational and career journeys, cultural and socio-economic backgrounds, we can never experience first-hand the institutional racism, microaggressions, prejudice, and discrimination experienced daily by our students of color.

Imagine a game of foosball being played on a table that is set up on a steep incline. Clearly, the player at the top of the hill benefits from gravity. All she needs to do is to gently flip back the ball to defend her goal, whereas the player at the bottom of the hill must work mightily and constantly to keep the ball from sliding through her goal. This description of institutional racism helps us see the uneven playing field created against people of color in our society.

One way of combating institutional racism is actively working to decrease the power differential between any in-group and out-group, including, for example, professors and students. Among the benefits of sharing power with students, Weimer includes more motivated students, better connection with the class content, a stronger sense of community, and fewer classroom management issues (Weimer, 2013). Weimer offers concrete recommendations to reduce the inherent power differential, including:

- Allow students some decision-making power in your classes. For example, use a "cafeteria plan" that allows students to choose their assignments from a menu of choices, but still provides clear constraints, such as due dates or assignment length. Alternatively, keep assignments uniform but allow students to decide their own due dates to develop their time management skills.
- Let students set some classroom policies, including managing class tardiness and expectations for class participation, and how to encourage participation and discourage

over-participation. This policy helps disrupt the status quo. For example, researchers have found that an average of 92% of class comments were made by only five students (Howard & Henny, 1998). We want to ensure our classrooms challenge this reality so that the voices of every student can be heard.
- Encourage students to own the classroom. Rearrange chairs so that they no longer in neat rows facing the instructor. Give students control of the dry-erase makers so they can post ideas on the board.
- Work collaboratively to set an agenda for what class topics should be most emphasized. For example, "We need to cover these five topics today. Which of them should be our highest priority and biggest focus, given what you perceive to be the content area most relevant to your learning?" Questions such as these encourage self-monitoring of learning, a vital component to being a lifelong learner.

2. Challenging the Imposter Syndrome

To promote culturally competent learning, professors also need to intentionally confront the "Imposter Phenomenon" common among first year students. Imposter syndrome is most elevated in students' first year of school, be it college or graduate school (Cokley, McClain, Enciso, & Martinez, 2013). Feeling like an imposter is common among both majority and minority students and males as well as females (Castro, Jones, & Mirsalimi, 2004). However, some students are particularly at risk to feel like imposters. Students who experience a higher level of perceived minority status stress have a directly proportional higher impression of themselves as imposters. In other words, student who perceive themselves to be stereotyped, isolated, or experiencing microaggressions are more likely to feel that they "don't belong" in higher education.

Intersecting marginalization compounds the effects of the imposter syndrome (Cokley, McClain, Enciso, & Martinez, 2013). For example, a LGBTQ+ Black female is more likely to feel like an imposter than a cisgendered, heterosexual Black male. In general, minority female students are more at risk for feeling like imposters than minority male students. Many minority females share the sentiment that the university made a mistake in admitting them (Castro, Jones, & Mirsalimi, 2004). Students are most vulnerable to the effects of the imposter syndrome when they believe that they are the cause of their failures but not their successes, which is a common perspective among students of color due to institutional racism.

To combat these views, educators need to actively create environments that students perceive to be safe, fair, and nonjudgmental. In order to aid students in overcoming imposter syndrome, it will be helpful to:

- Vigilantly, directly, and continuously challenge the perceptions that students have of themselves as imposters. Even if this view is unstated, don't assume that it is not affecting students. Have frank conversations with students about how common the imposter syndrome is.
- Make deliberate efforts to reach out to students who may be particularly vulnerable to the imposter syndrome, such as students with intersecting marginalizing demographic characteristics, such as minority females or LGBTQ+ students of color.
- Remember that a lack of approach does not imply a lack of interest. Instead, students may be reluctant to volunteer or get involved in projects because they are struggling with feelings of phoniness. Consistent efforts to reach out to students over time are thus paramount: One invitation to participate is rarely sufficient.

3. Facilitating Meaningful Yet Difficult Conversations about Race

To create culturally competent learning environments requires us to risk enough to change the status quo of our current classrooms, and indeed challenge the very racist foundations on which our society was built. Although these dialogues are difficult to have, genuine conversations about race are exponentially effective tools that can be used to break down racist power structures (Sue, 2015). Some professors may wonder why they need to have conversations about race, given that they teach a class that "has nothing to do with race." For example, perhaps you teach classes in computer science, math, chemistry, or engineering. Given the technical and hard science nature of these classes, you might believe that issues of race and culture are not relevant to your subject matter. After all, the race of a student is irrelevant when a student balances a chemical equation or solves for the area of the triangle.

However, this philosophy is misguided. If race and gender did not affect the hard and computer sciences, then we would expect the percentages of individuals choosing these fields as careers to be roughly even across all college graduates. Indeed, we would expect roughly 50% of chemists, computer programmers, mathematicians, and computer scientists to be female and 50% to be male. We would also expect that the demographic composition of these professions would mirror our racially diverse society. Yet, only 6% of computer programmers are Black, only 2.6% of chemists are Latinx, and only 1% of mathematicians are Native American (Heylin, 2007; Lee & Mather, 2008; Mather, 2008).

The current statistics are even more disappointing when intersecting identities are considered. In fact, statistical data regarding intersectionality in the STEM fields proved almost impossible to find. For example, percentages of Black gay mathematicians or Asian-American females in computer programming would be expected to be low, but these figures are generally not known. The effects of intersectionality compound the already substantial effects of marginalization in an invalidating environment (Moradi & Subich, 2003). To give an example, a Black individual will experience stress related to political and societal power differentials. However, if that individual is Black and female, then the power differential expands proportionally, and that effect is compounded if the person is a Black female who identifies as

LGBTQ+. Thus, although marginalization negatively affects many individuals on a fundamental level, none of our higher education structures are doing much to control for this problem.

One significant issue that contributes to both the imposter syndrome and the low percentage of people of color in various professions is our historic minimization and exclusion of people of color as exemplars in our field. For example, we praise Albert Einstein, Steve Jobs, Aristotle, and George Washington but ignore Rebecca Lee Crumpler (first Black female physician), Benjamin Banneker (land surveyor vital to designing Washington DC), Frederick McKinley (inventor of refrigerated trucks) and Dr. Shirley Ann Jackson (physicist). This example of covert racism is maintained out of convenience—we are less familiar with the contributions of people of color in our respective fields. This invisibility serves to maintain the illusion that people of color did not contribute to the advancement of society.

To visualize the concept of the erasure of people of color, imagine gradually climbing the academic ladder. As you reach each rung, you find fewer and fewer people who think, look, and act like you. Instead, each classroom, laboratory, internship, and research project is increasingly populated by people who you have traditionally faced as persecutors. Imagine the stress and anxiety that such an invalidating and unfamiliar environment would cause an individual. Now imagine that distress being compounded with every layer of marginalized identity added to the equation. Naturally, students vulnerable to such a phenomenon are more likely to be psychologically affected by the doubts surrounding their own self-efficacy (Cokley, McClain, Enciso, & Martinez, 2013).

However, starting a private conversation about race, and supporting students in doing so, is a powerful way of disarming the power of such doubts. If we fail to open meaningful dialogues about our differences, (even in classes that seemingly have "nothing to do with race") then we are only aggravating the previously mentioned dilemma of the tipped foosball table. In fact, in fields with such a preponderance of white men, the foosball table might be considered particularly uneven. To a person of color with several layers of intersectionality, it may as well be mounted on the highest peaks of the Himalayas with a frightening vertical descent.

This is why race talks are so important in the classroom. To ensure that students are entering our professional fields in proportions that represent our census data, we need to talk about how issues of race, privilege, microaggressions, and culture permeate our lives every day. Why is it important to talk about these tough issues? Because 63% of students of color report regularly experiencing microaggressions in academic settings (Boysen, 2012). For example, 63% of students of color reported regularly experiencing microaggressions in academic settings (Boysen, 2012). Equally appalling, 44% of students of color report experiencing not just microaggressions, but more overt racist behaviors in their classrooms, perpetuated by both their colleagues and professors (Boysen, 2012). Consequently, the cumulative effect of these microaggressions and overt racist behaviors has been found to have a highly aversive effect on student engagement and academic performance (Boysen, 2012).

Derald Wing Sue, the premier expert in the field of multiculturalism, suggests that educators should lead meaningful classroom discussions around race to combat the toxic effects of institutional racism (Sue, 2015). Self-reflective discussions about race are one of the most effective tools to help create a path to mutual respect and understanding. These conversations are often difficult, because we must recognize, and admit, our own biases and how we are products of cultural conditioning. Authentic conversations require directly dealing with White student and professor guardedness that results from denying and minimizing the effects of racism, sexism, and other biases. To be successful, professors must be willing to be vulnerable enough to model honesty, even in admitting our own biases, so that conversations about race do not become stilted and ineffective (Sue, 2015).

When I (Wohlfarth) have had these conversations about race in my classrooms, they typically engender student reactions that range from annoyance to anger. No one is left happy and satisfied. Perhaps this lack of success reflects deficits in my own teaching skills; perhaps it reflects a lack of reflection in understanding my own biases and thus demonstrating vulnerability. Although an overgeneralization, I would summarize students' responses after conversations about race as follows: White students leave the classroom grumpy, reluctant to admit their own racial biases, and overwhelmed at being asked to meaningfully consider the many benefits of white privilege. White students would rather "focus on the content matter" instead of undergoing the painful self-reflection that comes with examining race. Students of color are often equally frustrated by the conversations. They are annoyed with their White colleagues who "don't get it." They are tired of combating daily racism, and exhausted by the constant pressure to speak up to challenge the unfair status quo. Having conversations about race can be overwhelming to students of color as they cannot ignore the issue—they will still be Black/Latino/Native when they leave the classroom. As one student said, "Racism is the only America I know."

The fact that students are frustrated, my student course evaluations suffer, and I myself am exhausted when I facilitate conversations about race will not deter me. I will still lead such conversations about race, and, equally important, weave ideas about race, culture, gender, socio-economic status, sexual orientation, and privilege through my day-by-day coverage of the course content. Teaching a class void of conversations about race means maintaining the status quo and allow institutional racism to flourish. My solution is to remain open to new ideas through reading books and listening to "others," reflect on my own biases and racial journey, and request and thoughtfully consider student feedback about my teaching. The recommendations regarding facilitating meaningful discussions about race are thus:

- Educate yourself about racial issues. Derald Wing Sue's excellent *Race Talk and the Conspiracy of Silence* (Sue, 2015) is a terrific starting point. Attend multi-cultural conferences both in your field and in higher education.
- Seek to understand how issues of race, privilege and racism interact with the subject matter you teach.

- Constantly explore your own cultural journey and examine your own biases. Be willing to admit these biases, even if they appall you, and actively work to change them. One of the best ways to challenge our own biases is to seek meaningful conversation and relationships with those who we identify as different than ourselves.
- Have the courage to facilitate authentic conversations about race in your classroom, even if the conversations are difficult. Change is hard for everyone, but change means people are learning, and that is our ultimate goal for students, and for ourselves.

4. Building Authentic Cross-Cultural Relationships

Building relationships with students is one of the most proven ways to motivate them to engage in our classes and actually learn. Parker Palmer's seminal book, *The Courage to Teach,* (Palmer, 2007) has one central message: Relationships matter. Parker discusses the importance of "relational trust" as being central to learning. Parker uses the term relational trust as a broad, all-encompassing term, which includes relationships between not only students and teachers, but teachers and teachers, and teachers and administrators. Ponder that idea for a minute: Parker means that high degrees of trust, good communication, and low turnover contribute to student achievement. Moreover, relational trust includes the difficult-to-measure qualities of compassion, patience, empathy, commitment, the capacity to forgive, and even the word we rarely use in academia: love.

To support this contention, Palmer cites a landmark study by Anthony Bryk and Barbara Schneider of Chicago K-12 schools (Palmer, 2007). This study specifically examined the correlation between students' gains in learning, as measured by standardized tests, and trusting relationships, as measured by teacher survey data. The results were powerful. Schools that reported strong relational trust were three times more likely to show improvements in math and reading than schools with weak relational trust scores. Furthermore, schools with low relational trust across several years had virtually no chance of improving students' math or reading scores over time. Parker's compelling book builds on this hypothesis. High level budgets, huge endowments, and fancy equipment do not matter near as much to student learning as building a community where people trust each other and work together well (Palmer, 2007).

The importance of relationships extends to college students as well. A positive relationship between students and professors improves student productivity as well as academic performance (Decker, Dona, & Christenson, 2007; Toldson, Braithwaite, & Rentie, 2009). Students are more engaged, work harder, and produce more quality work when they perceive their professors care about them. To underscore this effect, Umbach and Wawrzynski (2005) found that students who reported more positive interactions with their professors were more likely to get involved in higher education endeavors such as research projects.

In advice to building relationship with students, we offer the following suggestions:

- Seek to build relationship with students who are ethnically, racially, and otherwise demographically different than you. Although cross-racial and cross-gender friendships can be complex and create misunderstandings, they can also be rewarding and lead to personal growth. Be steadfast in your attempts to build a bridge between yourself and students from varying backgrounds. They may need these relationships more than you could ever imagine.
- Pay close attention to the cultural values, including differences in philosophical systems, such as Eastern vs. Western ideas that are held by yourself and your students. Watch for the tendency to reify your own values while disparaging others. For example, my (Wohlfarth) German ancestry is likely a component in my hyper-punctuality and efficiency, so I need to actively work not to judge students too harshly when they are a few minutes late to a meeting.
- Share the story of how you became a teacher and/or how you fell in love with the subject matter you teach. Parker

(2007) particularly nudges us to share our professional mistakes and academic dead-ends. In sharing our mistakes, we teach students powerful lessons about being able to overcome challenges and setbacks, and still achieve valuable roles in society.

- Know that building relationships with students of color may take more time if a professor is White. Institutional racism has a powerful grip, and it may leave students of color wary and mistrustful of those in power. As a faculty person, you represent such power.
- Being an ally to your students does not simply mean building a relationship with them, but also creating a safe environment. The covert marginalizing tendencies of your colleagues, and even your institution, may become more transparent as you begin building bridges with your multicultural students. If you are a White professor, you may start to see the unevenness in the foosball table as never before, which can lead to disillusionment. As you work through these feelings, you can begin to challenge institutional racism on a more systemic level.

5. Supporting Students when They are "The Only"

With the notable exception of HBCUs (Historically Black Colleges and Universities) and TCUs (Tribal Colleges and Universities), students of color have been historically and remain currently underrepresented in other American colleges and universities. Because of this underrepresentation, the chances are high that you, as a professor, may have a classroom where you have an "only," such as a single Black man in a class of 32 other white students, or a single Native student in a class of 75 other white students.

We (Harris and Joseph) have often been in classes as "the only," including being the only male, but also being the only Black person, making us doubly different than our peers in a room full of White women. Furthermore, our professors are also likely to be either White women or White males. Now, imagine that everyone in the class is sharing their understanding of the course content. Everyone takes their turn in sharing and then "the only" speaks, and the conversation involves race for the first time. Why was the topic of race obscured before "the only" brought it to the attention of the class? Why hadn't the professor brought up the relationship between race and the course content?

Even more challenging, "the only" has the unfair burden of representing all people of their gender, race, ethnicity, sexual orientation, gender identity status, socio-economic background, religion, nationality, or immigrant status. Imagine how difficult it would be for you to speak for the beautiful heterogeneity of all people who share your race or gender, but we put even more of a burden on "the only." Indeed, every time issues of race, culture or ethnicity are discussed in class, all eyes turn to "the only" not just as the expert on his or her race, but on the entire topic of multi-culturalism. Thus, we can easily make the following erroneous assumptions: 1) only students of color have a culture; 2) only students of color are qualified to be multi-cultural experts; and 3) all students of color are indeed multicultural experts.

Thus, in any classroom situation in which we have "the only," we need to take extra steps to manage classroom dynamics so they do not become unintentionally stifling. The following suggestions may be helpful:

- Meet with "the only" student outside of class, to listen to his or her perspectives on the classroom dynamics and how these dynamics might affect the student. Ask the student for suggestions on how they could best be supported.
- Have a frank conversation with the class on the first day of class regarding the gender, cultural, sexual, and racial differences in the class. Point out the erroneous assumptions listed above and ask students what they might do, as a class, to counteract these beliefs.
- Check in regularly with "the only" throughout the semester, to understand the classroom dynamics from his/her/their unique perspective. Ideally, these meetings would be in your office and over a cup of tea, instead of a pub-

lic, 2-minute conversation as students file out after class in which you hurriedly ask the student if "everything is going OK."

6. Practicing Cultural Humility to Build Truly Collaborative Classrooms

A great deal of emphasis has been placed on the idea of cultural competence, or having the knowledge, skills, and attitudes to interact with others from cultures different than one's own. The authors of this chapter agree that striving for cultural competence is a worthwhile endeavor. However, we also share the opinion of researchers such as Hook, Watkins, Davis, Owen, Van Tongeren, & Ramos (2016) that cultural competence cannot be a true endpoint. The main problem with the concept of cultural competence is that it is a myth, for one can never truly achieve an endpoint of being culturally competent. First, no one can ever learn the all-encompassing cultural knowledge, values, ways of knowing, ways of being, customs, and languages represented by the diverse customs of the world. Second, even if this level of competence were theoretically possible, all cultures are constantly changing, growing, merging, and/or dying. Culture is dynamic, and so our encyclopedic knowledge would be perpetually outdated. Third, one cannot ever completely know one's self because we are always growing and changing. Even if we came to understand our privileges, values, cultural biases, prejudices, stereotypes, and cultural background, we could still be challenged by new information that we had not yet encountered. Fourth, assuming that we can become truly culturally competent is a worrisome construct, perhaps the ultimate assumption of privilege. How would we know that we truly had achieved cultural competence?

To deal with these inherent problems of the concept of cultural competence, Tervalon and Murray-Garcia (1998) have contrasted the idea with cultural humility. Tervalon and Murray-Garcia (1998) proposed that cultural humility is the ability to maintain an interpersonal position that is other-oriented in relation to the cultural identity most salient to that individual. Unlike the idea of cultural competence, cultural humility suggests that we must always be tentative in our knowledge, are perpetually on a cultural journey, and open to new others and experiences as we come from a place of "not knowing." This is difficult for us, perhaps particularly so since we are professors and thus place a high priority on knowing our content areas, being certain in our presentation, confident in our answers, and expert at hiding our weaknesses. Not knowing, and being OK with never being able to fully know, but yet continuing our search anyway is a difficult and tentative place within our universe. It is a place of fuzzy borders and shades of gray, of accepting life's inconsistencies, and constantly re-evaluating one's place in the word.

Such introspective journeying is difficult. Yet consider this: In such a messy place of fuzzy borders, we are constantly open to change as we come in contact with new others, ideas, and experiences. Consider an analogy of watercolor painting, with the artist painting the blue before the yellow is dry, and suddenly, the painting bleeds rich with thousands of shades of nuanced greens—mossy greens, turquoise blue greens, golden greens, mint greens, emerald greens, seafoam greens, forest greens—more shades of green than we ever thought possible, blurring into shapes that we didn't plan to draw yet that contribute to the overall beauty of the painting. In those messy edges, true collaboration, in which we learn to listen to one another instead of just speak, becomes at last a possibility. In that true collaboration comes the absolute joy of learning *with* each other. Our goal is to know the research the best we can, including its limitations, and move forward in hopes of creating such meaningful opportunities to learn together.

References

Boysen, G. A. (2012). Teacher and student perceptions of microaggressions in college classrooms. *College Teaching, 60,* 122-129. doi: 10.1080/87567555.2012.654831.

Bryk, A. & Schneider, B. (2007). As cited in Palmer, P. (2007). *The Courage to Teach: Exploring the Inner Landscape of a Teacher's Life.* Jossey-Bass: San Francisco.

Castro, D. M., Jones, R. A., & Mirsalimi, H. (2004). Parentification and the impostor phenomenon: An empirical investigation. *The American Journal of Family Therapy, 32*(3), 205-216.

Cokley, K., McClain, S., Enciso, A., & Martinez, M. (2013). An examination of the impact of minority status stress and impostor feelings on the mental health of diverse ethnic minority college students. *Journal of Multicultural Counseling and Development, 41*(2), 82-95

Decker, D. M., Dona, D. P., & Christenson, S. L. (2007). Behaviorally at-risk African American students: The importance of student–teacher relationships for student outcomes. *Journal of School Psychology, 45*(1), 83-109.

Heylin, M. (2007). ACS News. Retrieved March 11, 2017, from http://pubs.acs.org/cen/email/html/cen_85_i38_8538acsnews.html.

Hook, J., Watkins, C., Davis, D., Owen, J., Van Tongeren, D., & Ramos, M. (2016). Cultural humility in psychotherapy supervision. *American Journal of Psychotherapy, 70(2),* 149-168.

Howard, J. & Henny, A. (1998). Student participation and instructor gender in the mixed-age classroom. *Journal of Higher Education, 69(4*), 384-405.

Kena, G., Hussar, W., McFarland, J., de Brey, C., Musu-Gillette, L., Wang, X., & Barmer, A. (2016). The Condition of Education 2016. NCES 2016-144. *National Center for Education Statistics*.

Lee, M., & Mather, M. (2008). *US labor force trends* (Vol. 63, No. 2). Population Reference Bureau.

Lin, L., Nigrinis, A., Christidis, P., & Stamm, K. (2015). Demographics of the US.

Mather, M. (2008). 2007 Occupational Profiles Reveal Wide Gender, Racial Gaps in Science and Engineering Employment. Retrieved March 11, 2017, from http://www.prb.org/Publications/Articles/2008/sloanoccupationpages.aspx.

Moradi, B., & Subich, L. M. (2003). A concomitant examination of the relations of perceived racist and sexist events to psychological distress for African American women. *The Counseling Psychologist, 31*(4), 451-469.

Palmer, P. J. (2007). *The Courage to Teach: Exploring the Inner Landscape of a Teacher's Life.* Jossey-Bass: San Francisco.

Richmond, A., Slattery, J., Mitchell, N., Morgan, R., & Becknell, J. (2016). Can a learner-centered syllabus change students' perceptions of student-professor rapport and master teacher behaviors? *Scholarship of Teaching and Learning in Psychology, 2(3),* 159-168.

Sue, D. W. (2015). *Race talk and the conspiracy of silence.* Wiley: Hoboken, NJ.

Tervalon, M., & Murray-Garcia, J. (1998). Cultural humility versus cultural competence: a critical distinction in defining physician training outcomes in multicultural education. *Journal of Health Care for the Poor and Underserved, 9(2),* 117-125.

Toldson, I. A., Braithwaite, R. L., & Rentie, R. J. (2009). Promoting college aspirations among school-age African American males. *African American males in higher education: Research, programs and academe diversity in higher education*, 117-137.

Trigwell, K. (2010) Teaching and learning: A relational view. In J.C. Hughes and J. Mighty (eds.) *Taking Stock: Research on Teaching and Learning in Higher*

Education. Montreal and Kingston: Queen's Policy Studies, McGill-Queen's University Press.

Umbach, P. D., & Wawrzynski, M. R. (2005). Faculty do matter: The role of college faculty in student learning and engagement. *Research in Higher Education, 46*(2), 153-184.

Weimer, M. (2013). *Learner-Centered Teaching: Five Key Changes to Practice.* Jossey-Bass: San Francisco.

Chapter Two

Understanding The Impact of and Addressing Classroom Microaggressions

By RoShunna Lea, Catherine Burke, Adriana Peña, Jimmy Joseph, & DeDe Wohlfarth

The presence of microaggressions in classrooms has been well researched (Solorzano, Ceja, & Yosso, 2000; Yosso, Smith, Ceja, & Solorzano, 2009; Boysen, 2012). Experiencing microaggressions can lead to negative social, emotional, and performance outcomes for minority students. Though prevalent, several research findings provide effective strategies for educators, students, and organizations to address classroom microaggressions and their impact. For professors, strategies include becoming more knowledgeable about multicultural issues and having open conversations when classroom microaggressions occur. For students, strategies include creating counter spaces and developing trusting relationships with academic mentors. Organizational strategies include the development of therapeutic communities and restructuring policies to create more supportive environments for all students.

Microaggressions are common in our classrooms, and research over the last two decades has supported just how pervasive the problem is (Solorzano, Ceja, & Yosso, 2000; Yosso, Smith, Ceja, & Solorzano, 2009; Boysen, 2012). Microaggressions are equally likely to occur in undergraduate and graduate level classrooms (Ong, Wright, Espinosa, & Orfield, 2011), a discouraging fact as increased educational levels does not make people less likely to commit microaggressions. Microaggressions can take a variety of forms, including verbal and physical behaviors. The impact of these subtle, yet powerful, exchanges often leads to negative social, emotional, and academic performance outcomes (Sue, Lin, Torino, Capodilupo, & Rivera, 2009).

The inescapable of microaggressions, although discouraging, has provided a silver lining. Because of the widespread prevalence of microaggressions, studying them is fairly easy. Their commonness has given rise to several research-supported ways to effectively address microaggressions. The objective of this chapter is to provide a brief overview of the literature on microaggressions, discuss how microaggressions commonly transpire in college classrooms, and provide strategies to effectively address microaggressions. This chapter will conclude with providing recommendations for educators, students of color, and other marginalized students who frequently experience microaggressions. Recommendations for institutions are also shared.

Literature Review

Derald Wing Sue (2013) defines microaggressions as expressions of subtle bias. These brief, common exchanges send demeaning messages to individuals solely because they belong to an "out" group, or a race, ethnicity, culture or religion marginalized by society. Microaggressions can be verbal, nonverbal, or visual and often occur automatically, or without any apparent conscious thought. Sue notes three subtypes of microaggressions: microassaults (direct verbal attacks on a person due to a demographic group), microinsults (actions that demean a person based on group membership or group status), and microinvalidations (behavior that denies the experience of minorities). Individuals can be targeted with microaggressions because of their race, ethnicity, gender, sexual orientation, gender expression, religion, or other variables. An important caveat should be added to this literature review in that the research on microaggressions is still in its infancy. Thus, stronger scientific data is needed to allow for more confidence in the information shared in this chapter.

Microaggressions in the Classroom

Approximately 65% of minority students report experiencing some type of prejudice or subtle bias on a college campus (Biasco, Goodwin, & Vitale, 2001). Even more disappointingly, college students report that the most common place they have experienced microaggressions or prejudiced behavior is in their classrooms.

Researchers have begun to explore the specific microaggressive experiences of students. Solorzano, Ceja, and Yosso (2000) conducted focus group interviews of African American students across three universities to explore their experiences of microaggressions in college classrooms. These students noted that they often felt invisible in class. They also believed that their needs were not as important as White students because they were outnumbered by majority student classmates. Minority students also reported feeling as though the faculty members held a consistently low expectation of them, which eventually led to feelings of self-doubt. Additionally, these students reported experiences of racial segregation in class study groups, which often increased their sense of social isolation. Overall, the classroom experiences of African American students contributed to feelings of despondency and fatigue that led to defensiveness and eventually impacted their academic performance.

McCabe (2009) conducted a similar study on the types of microaggressions likely to be experienced by male and female minority members representing various racial groups on college campuses. Using focus group interview data from these individuals, McCabe found specific patterns of microaggressions that were individual to unique demographic groups as well as common themes of microaggressions commonly experienced by all marginalized students. African American men experienced more microaggressions around campus and in social settings than African American women, who reported more biases in their classrooms.

Students also reported feeling frustrated that they were expected to be the spokespeople for their entire gender or racial group. For example, if the class discussion focused on a racial topic, some professors directly asked for the opinion of the minority student on the issue. Experiences like these sometimes left the minority individuals with the sense that they were different from, and thus isolated from, their classmates. Students further noted that they felt particularly isolated if they were the sole minority person of their group in a classroom because they were the only voice that could speak for an entire group. McCabe (2009) noted that this "burden of representation" is a common feeling among minority students at primarily White institutions. A more encouraging finding from McCabe's (2009) research is that many minority students, after several occasions of being the only minority in a classroom, began to embrace their positions of minority spokesperson and appreciated the opportunity to have open dialogue with their classmates. In short, they viewed these conversations, however awkwardly they had begun, as at least a chance to discuss the role of race in relation to the course content.

Dialogue and Response to Microaggressions

Given that microaggressions are so common in the classroom, an important consideration is not *if* professors will need to address them in their classrooms, but *when* they will need to do so. A wide variety of responses are possible, of course, but the most likely professor responses to microaggressions are to do nothing or minimize the situation. A better outcome than doing nothing is to have a dialogue, even if the dialogue is difficult (Sue, Lin, Torino, Capodilupo, & Rivera, 2009). Dialogue in the moment, despite its potential awkwardness, is one of the most effective ways of addressing microaggressions, but such dialogues must be handled with care. The ideal conversation is one that allows both parties to be heard in the guiding and validating presence of an instructor. However, the professor must not allow students, whether perpetrators or victims of microaggressions, to deny or minimize the role of racism in our society (Boysen, 2012).

The most common microaggressions center around particular themes (Sue et al., 2009). Common microaggressions include ascriptions of the etiology of intelligence, alien in one's own land, the denial of racial realities and institutional racism, and assumptions of criminality (Sue et al, 2009). *Ascriptions of the etiology of intelligence* occur when White individuals attribute a particular degree of intelligence to students of color. For example, students may automatically assume that an Asian male student will excel at statistics and that an African American female student will struggle with the same topic. *Alien in one's own land* microaggressions occur when White individuals make statements that depict certain individuals as perpetually foreign. For example, students may comment that a person's "English is really good" or ask a minority student where s/he is "from."

Incidents involving a *denial of racial reality and denial of institutional racism* often trigger the most difficult dialogue in classrooms because the racial reality of the student of color is dismissed or invalidated. These microaggressions are elucidated by comments such as: "Not everything is about race," "Don't you think you're being a little sensitive?" "Perhaps you're misinterpreting the situation," or "Do we have to play the race card again?". Another example of this type of microaggression is when White students insist they are "colorblind" and do not "see color, only individuals" or argue in the universality of the human experience, as in "We all bleed red." These statements deny the continuing impact of institutional racism in the lives of people of color.

The *assumption of criminality* theme occurs when White students attribute violence to African American students. For example, students may perceive violence and anger in people of color more so than in fellow White students. An example of this common microaggression might be when a White student tells a Black student not to get so "hostile" and "loud" in classroom discussions. Comments such as these serve to perpetuate stereotypes of people of color as dangerous and violent.

When incidents such as these occur in a classroom, professors should not ignore them (Sue, 2013; 2016). Instead, they should lead the class in a conversation about the statements made and their impact on people of color. Professors should utilize a direct approach in managing classroom discussions, being firm and clear in their willingness to intervene. Professors benefit by being comfortable with such race talk themselves, although achieving this ideal takes time and practice, like any other skill.

Impact on Students

One question that professors may be asking themselves is if intervening to stop and process a microaggression is worth the time and distraction from class content. It seems the easier option would be to just pretend we didn't see or hear the problematic exchange, or to respond with a bland, "We need to get back to covering the course content." We may even convince ourselves that we can always intervene next time if a microaggression is perpetrated. Or we can try to deny or minimize the impact of such microaggressions on students, believing that our sticking to the coverage of the course content is far more important than dealing with students' "hurt feelings."

However, ignoring microaggressions leads to detrimental outcomes. Some of these long-term negative outcomes have already been discussed, but it is worthwhile to slow down and consider what happens to students "in the moment" after a microaggression occurs. First, the minority student is likely to experience a range of immediate reactions that include negative cognitive, behavioral, and emotional responses (Sue et al., 2009).

Cognitive reactions can include having to quickly balance the desire to speak honestly about certain issues with the fear of possible consequences for that honesty. Immediately post-microaggression, students of color engage in an internal debate about if responding is worth it, and, if so, how to respond. McCabe (2009) notes that commonly considered responses by minority students after a microaggression include responding with a sense of humor or giving perpetrators the benefit of the doubt.

Behavioral reactions on behalf of minority students can include acting a certain way in the classroom to be accepted by others. Many minority students develop "thick skin" and a high threshold of painful and ignorant comments before they react. Conversely, some minority students become hyper-sensitive to the microaggressive behavior and the comments of their White classmates. The constant decision making in regards to reacting to microaggressions, in addition to the negative experience of the microaggression itself, takes a psychological toll on minority students. Managing these complex feelings on a daily basis can result in anger, anxiety, and exhaustion. When regularly occurring, these negative emotions increase the likelihood of the minority students experiencing psychological trauma (McCabe, 2009).

In a study specifically focusing on racial trauma, Pieterse, Carter, Evans, and Walter (2010) explored the relationship between trauma, discrimination, and the overall racial climate of the college. They found that minority students' perception of discrimination was associated with trauma-related symptoms, including intrusive thoughts, nightmares, and irritability for Black students. The likelihood of a student experiencing trauma symptoms was also correlated with the overall racial climate of the university, with negative college climates producing more racial traumatic experiences for students of color. In summary, both the short and long-term mental health of our students of color demands that professors intervene in the moment when microaggressions occur, despite the temptation to ignore such problematic behavior.

Research has shown that microaggressions impact White students as well. Although White students are less often studied in regards to the effects of microaggressions in the classroom setting, they, too, can be negatively impacted by these behaviors (Spanierman, Poteat, Beer, & Armstrong, 2006). Common problems for White students include receiving messages that such microaggressive behavior is acceptable. Additionally, not intervening to stop a microaggression leads to a lack of awareness in being able to identify microaggressions. Furthermore, not dealing with microaggressions tends to decrease empathy and lower compassion of White students towards students of color. This dimming of perceptual awareness allows White students to remain clueless about the role of privilege in their lives as well as make it more likely that they will continue to engage in microaggressions, usually without any awareness that they are doing so.

Recommendations for Professors

1. Faculty members often struggle significantly with addressing racial tension in the classroom (Sue et al., 2009). Although our discomfort is likely an honest reflection of broader societal conflicts about racial issues, our responses of ignoring, silence, joking, or half-hearted interventions lead to students of color feeling invalidated and silenced in class. Derald Wing Sue's book, *Race Talks: Conspiracy of Silence* (Sue, 2016) provides an excellent framework for educators to become comfortable addressing classroom microaggressions. The book includes a step-by-step process for instructors to facilitate difficult conversations about race.

2. Although racial discussions can be difficult for instructors to navigate, they are easier to facilitate when the classroom expectations around microaggressions have been expressed before transgressions occur. Thus, professors should begin each course with an open conversation about microaggressions and their impact as well as share the classroom policy regarding the occurrence of microaggressions. The first day of class may also be a good time for educators to discuss the common response of fear in addressing microaggressions and normalize reactions of initial discomfort. Having this conversation helps alleviate minority students' common concern that they will be perceived as "easily offended." Additionally, early dialogue is the ideal time to discuss compassion and empathy, including both self-compassion and compassion for others, even when ruptures occur.

3. Given the current sociopolitical climate, students may feel afraid to approach a student or professor about a microaggression due to fears of being labeled as problematic, combative, too sensitive, misinterpreting, or confused. If a student has the courage to bring up a microaggression that occurred in the classroom with a professor, either by another student or by the professor, we must remain non-defensive in our reactions, despite the difficulty in

doing so. Also, genuinely praising the student who has brought up a microaggression is encouraged. If a student feels offended or upset, try to repair the rupture as amicably and honestly as possible. After discussing the microaggression with the student, ask the student for feedback to ensure that everyone involved is satisfied and all messages were received as intended (Boysen, 2012). This can be an uncomfortable process, but is necessary for the growth and success of all involved.

4. Instructors value their work and appreciate the difference they are making in the world via their students. Solid relationships between students and professors strengthen this impact. If a major or repeated rupture occurs between a student and faculty member, the professor should reach out to support the student given the inherent power differential between students and professors. Professors need to be comfortable in accepting that their reality may be different than the reality of a student of a marginalized group, even if the two individuals share racial or ethnic similarities. Open and honest dialogues create beneficial spaces for professors to learn alternate perspectives as well as connect with their students on a deeper level, thus increasing their multicultural awareness.

5. Research has found certain strategies to be unhelpful when discussing microaggressions in the classroom (Sue, 2009). Specifically, Sue suggests avoiding being passive and letting the students challenge the microaggressive behavior, being dismissive or disengaged from the conversation, minimizing the experiences of minority students, and placing students of color in the role of racial expert.

Recommendations for Students

1. African American students who created and participated in academic and social "counter spaces" (i.e. fraternities, sororities, study groups) experienced more cultural, emotional, and academic support than those who did not (Solorzano, Ceja & Yosso, 2000). More specifically, participation in counter spaces validated their

experiences of microaggressions in a supportive environment with others who had gone through similar incidents.

2. Likewise, Yosso, Smith, Ceja, and Solórzano (2009) found that Latina/o students commonly responded to microaggressions by building academic and social counter spaces, including participating in Latina/o community events, preparing culturally authentic meals, and reading Spanish language books. Students also sought out Latina/o studies classes to create academic counter spaces, which helped them see themselves as part of a legacy that resisted oppression. In addition to mitigating negative impacts of microaggressions such as extreme stress, a lost sense of control, confusion, and ambiguity, participating in these activities helped students learn to navigate multiple worlds, develop high self-expectations and a strong work ethic, and succeed despite the racism they experienced.

3. Research has shown that establishing a trusting relationship with an academic mentor who is sensitive to multicultural issues can be a protective factor for minority students (Alvarez, Blume, Cervantes & Thomas, 2009). Appropriate mentors will help minority students develop crucial skills such as learning the culture of academia, reflecting on the personal impact of belonging to multiple worlds and having multiple identities, and developing coping skills to deal with future instances of discrimination in the academic setting.

Recommendations for Organizations

1. Racial microaggressions are often embedded in the hierarchical system of power and organizational culture (Solorzano, Ceja, & Yosso, 2000; Yosso et al., 2009). Thus, adopting an organizational framework that supports students who experience long-term stress and adversity is crucial. One framework that may be helpful is "The Sanctuary Model" (Esaki, Benamati, Yanosy, Middleton, Hopson, Hummer, & Bloom, 2013). This trauma-focused model is based in systems theory and posits that institutions should develop more validating communities in order to provide high levels of support to individuals exposed to adversity.

These high levels of support will eventually lead to the creation of institutions with restorative cultures that counteract the effects of social and psychological trauma.

2. In research designed to explore the impact of microaggressions on a broader, institutional level, Allen, Scott, and Lewis (2013) concluded that schools should provide culturally affirming education to limit the negative social, psychological, and intellectual outcomes of minority students. They suggest a restructuring of discipline policies and academic tracking to address high levels of racial disparities. They also suggest a transition from hegemonic, universal curricula to more culturally specific and empowering course content. Integrating race and cultural consciousness into the education process will lead to more culturally affirming classrooms.

Exercises

Vignette/Example 1

Tyrone is a 19-year-old male of Caribbean descent. He is a first-generation American and is currently enrolled in a literature course at a large Southern university where he is one of only two Black students. Tyrone feels particularly drained whenever he leaves his literature class. Today, his class is discussing their reactions to the latest assigned reading, *Things Fall Apart*, a novel about European colonialism in an African village. Tyrone's professor begins class by looking at Tyrone and directly asks, "Tyrell, what were your thoughts on this book?" Tyrone sighed. "It's Tyrone, actually," he said, correcting his professor for the tenth time in three weeks about his name.

His professor laughed. "Sorry. I don't know why I'm having such a hard time remembering. What did you think of the book? I would like to get a Black perspective." Tyrone reluctantly shared his perspective and was complimented by his professor for "being so articulate." Tyrone thought this was odd, as he noticed that the professor never complimented other students on their language usage. As other classmates began sharing their perspectives, Tyrone noted that a few of them felt that the colonists "helped" the African characters by "civilizing" them and introducing them to Christianity. As he walked out of class, one classmate approached him and asked what part of Africa he was from and if anything in the book had ever happened to any of his ancestors. Tyrone shook his head and left the class, disgusted.

Reflection Questions:
1. What types of microaggressions did you notice and who perpetrated them?
2. How could you, as a professor, have attempted to evoke Tyrone's perspective on the book in a more culturally empowering manner?
3. How would you have guided the classroom discussion about "civilizing" Africans?
4. What emotional, cognitive, and behavioral responses did you notice in the vignette? How do you think these responses are likely to evolve as Tyrone returns to his dorm and reflects on the class discussion?
5. How do you think Tyrone will respond to his fellow students and to the professor during future class discussions?

Vignette/Example 2

Jeremy is a 21-year-old White male currently finishing his last year of community college. Alyssa is a 25-year-old Japanese American female at the same community college. They are in the same biology class and sit at the same table. The biology professor began the course with a conversation about diversity and how to be sensitive to differences in the classroom. During this particular class period, the professor asked the students to form small groups to work on the assignment. Jeremy immediately leaned forward and stated loudly, "I want Alyssa on my team. The Chinese are like math and science geniuses. I read that they make them study like 12 hours a day in China."

The professor overheard this and immediately stopped all of the students from moving about the room and forming groups in order to address the comment. She stated, "Do you all remember us talking about microaggressions at the beginning of the semester? This is exactly what I was talking about." Alyssa shifted in her chair uncomfortably. Jeremy rolled his eyes and said, "Oh my gosh. I was complimenting her. Everyone gets so offended over everything nowadays! You can't even compliment someone anymore!" The professor disagreed, but noting that the class time was almost over, she told both students to come to her office during office hours if they wanted to discuss the incident further. Neither student ever went to her office.

Reflection Questions:

1. *What types of microaggressions did you notice in the scenario?*
2. *How do you think the professor could have handled the situation more effectively?*
3. *What were some positive aspects of how the professor handled the situation?*
4. *Do you think the professor's actions will impact Jeremy's future attitudes and behaviors?*
5. *What were likely some of Alyssa's emotional and cognitive reactions to this incident and how do you think this incident will affect her future classroom behavior?*

Conclusion

Microaggressions are pervasive both in academic settings and the world at large. However, microaggressions are not an unavoidable aspect of life. Societies can and do change, but only because the people who live in those societies intentionally change them. The desire to receive an advanced degree should be applauded and encouraged in every manner possible. Attaining an education should not leave any individual students with feelings of low self-worth, isolation, frustration, and the psychological and emotional scars of trauma.

Professors play a vital role in ensuring that all students are supported in our classroom. In order to do this, we must continually educate ourselves on the detrimental impact of microaggressions in the classroom and how we can decrease their occurrence. Though microaggressions may seem like a harmless "slips of the tongue" or we may not notice them at all, these words and actions are just one more example of the long line of discriminatory acts that minority individuals have faced. We cannot control the actions of everyone, but we can work to create classrooms that are safe, healthy spaces for all students.

References

Allen, A., Scott, L. M., & Lewis, C. W. (2013). Racial Microaggressions and African American and Hispanic students in urban schools: A call for culturally affirming education. *Interdisciplinary Journal of Teaching and Learning, 3*(2), 117-129.

Alvarez, A. N., Blume, A. W., Cervantes, J. M., & Thomas, L. R. (2009). Tapping the wisdom tradition: Essential elements to mentoring students of color. *Professional Psychology: Research and Practice, 40*(2), 181.

Biasco, F., Goodwin, E. A., & Vitale, K. L. (2001). College students' attitudes toward racial discrimination. *College Student Journal, 35*(4), 523-529.

Boysen, G. A. (2012). Teacher and student perceptions of microaggressions in college classrooms. *College Teaching, 60*(3), 122-129. doi:10.1080/87567555.2012.654831.

Esaki, N., Benamati, J., Yanosy, S., Middleton, J., Hopson, L., Hummer, V., & Bloom, S. (2013). The sanctuary model: Theoretical framework. *Families in Society: The Journal of Contemporary Social Services, 94*(2), 87-95.

McCabe, J. (2009). Racial and gender microaggressions on a predominantly-White campus: Experiences of Black, Latina/o and White undergraduates. *Race, Gender & Class*, 133-151.

Ong, M., Wright, C., Espinosa, L., & Orfield, G. (2011). Inside the double bind: A synthesis of empirical research on undergraduate and graduate women of color in science, technology, engineering, and mathematics. *Harvard Educational Review, 81*(2), 172-209.

Pieterse, A. L., Carter, R. T., Evans, S. A., & Walter, R. A. (2010). An exploratory examination of the associations among racial and ethnic discrimination, racial climate, and trauma-related symptoms in a college student population. *Journal of Counseling Psychology, 57*(3), 255.

Solorzano, D., Ceja, M., & Yosso, T. (2000). Critical race theory, racial microaggressions, and campus racial climate: The experiences of African American college students. *Journal of Negro Education*, 60-73.

Spanierman, L. B., Poteat, V. P., Beer, A. M., & Armstrong, P. I. (2006). Psychosocial costs of racism to whites: Exploring patterns through cluster analysis. *Journal of Counseling Psychology, 53*(4), 434.

Sue, D. W. (2013). Race talk: The psychology of racial dialogues. *American Psychologist, 68*(8), 663.

Sue, D. W. (2016). *Race talk and the conspiracy of silence: Understanding and facilitating difficult dialogues on race*. John Wiley & Sons.

Sue, D. W., Lin, A. I., Torino, G. C., Capodilupo, C. M., & Rivera, D. P. (2009). Racial microaggressions and difficult dialogues on race in the classroom. *Cultural Diversity and Ethnic Minority Psychology, 15*(2), 183-190. doi:10.1037/a0014191

Yosso, T., Smith, W., Ceja, M., & Solórzano, D. (2009). Critical race theory, racial microaggressions, and campus racial climate for Latina/o undergraduates. *Harvard Educational Review, 79*(4), 659-691.

Chapter Three

Cultural Competency: An Organizing Principle for Effective Partnerships Between Academic and Student Affairs

By Natalie A. Gibson

Student development theorists point to the importance of educating the whole student. Practically speaking, there is agreement that learning occurs through curricular and co-curricular endeavors. In this context, collaborative efforts that involve student affairs and academic affairs are critical. Often times effective partnerships are problematic due to different operating cultures between the two areas. Written for community college faculty, administrative and staff leaders, the following article explores these two cultures and offers cultural competence as a mechanism to help bridge the divide. This article concludes with an interactive exercise that helps unpack the cultural difference as an initial step for college leaders interested in establishing effective partnership between faculty and student affairs professionals.

Student learning occurs inside and outside the classroom. Many community colleges are seeking ways to create holistic learning environments where the curriculum and co-curriculum come together to support the overarching academic mission. Successful partnerships between academic affairs and student affairs however, are fraught with challenges. Gaps in the development, evolution, and function create structural and cultural divisions between the two functional areas that are often difficult to bridge. In order to address the cultural chasm, student services professionals and academic affairs faculty members can become culturally competent in order to address subcultural issues. This chapter will explore the use of cultural competency as a guiding principle for developing effective partnerships between student and academic affairs in the community college setting.

Contemporary Community College

More than 12 million students enrolled in 1,123 public and private community colleges in fall 2013 (American Association of Community Colleges, 2015). These enrollments represent 46% of all U.S. undergraduates. Given these numbers, community colleges are central (Dougherty, 2001) to the K-16 educational system. Community colleges are distinct in higher education for their open door admissions policy. Community colleges provide access to all students who want to engage in postsecondary education (Nevarez & Wood, 2010).

Community colleges value teaching. According to Nevarez & Wood (2010), teaching is an influential core value of community colleges that characterizes the purpose of these institutions. Vaughn (2006) comments, "the most important challenge for community college instructors is to develop the ability to adjust styles of teaching to the diverse learning styles of students" (p.7).

The community college open door philosophy suggests "a clear obligation to do the best for everyone" (McCabe, 2003, p. 12) admitted to enroll. Students who start at a community college are less likely to complete a credential or transfer to a four-year institution that those students who begin at the university (Bailey & Morest, 2006). Out of 100 first time students entering a community college, 15 will complete a degree or certificate within three years, while 45 will leave school without completing a credential (Provasnik & Planty, 2008). This outcome is a challenge that community colleges must address in the future as parents, students, business and decision makers at all levels of government are calling for higher levels of accountability for student success and completion.

One way to conceptualize these collaborative arrangements involves faculty members acting as guides to students who are actively engaged in their own learning (Weimer, 2012). An additional way to think about these collaborations involves partnerships between academic affairs and student affairs – the intentional integration of curriculum with the co-curriculum (Frost, Strom, Downey, Schultz, & Holland, 2010).

Theoretical Underpinnings

The work of theorists Astin (1983), Pasceralla and Terenzini (2005) as well as Tinto (1995) and Rendon (2001) support the integration of social and emotional student development in higher education. Collectively, their scholarly endeavors point out the need for colleges to educate the whole student. Institutions are encouraged to dissolve historic, persistent divisions of labor between faculty who attend to the students' intellectual development and student affairs professionals who focus on social and emotional development. A holistic approach to developing students undergirds the reality that student learning occurs both inside and outside the classroom. Consequently, student affairs and academic affairs units need each other (West Ed Group, 2012) to achieve a common goal of advancing intellectual and personal development of students (Arcelus, 2011).

Developing Academic-Student Affairs Partnerships

Successful partnerships between academic affairs and student affairs are fraught with challenges. According to Cross et.al (2010), barriers to successful partnerships include historic separation between curricular and co-curricular instruction and perceived second-class status of student affairs in the context of an academic mission. These units rarely coordinate efforts. The lack of coordination increases the likelihood of difficulty meeting the full spectrum of student needs (WestEd and PR group, 2012). Cultural distinctions between academic affairs and student affairs also limit the quest for cross-functional partnerships (Arcelus, 2011 and Cross et al., 2010). The historic and persistent gaps in development, evolution, and function create structural and cultural divisions that are often difficult to bridge. Educators within student services and academic affairs have opportunity to become culturally competent in order to address subcultural issues identified in order to develop effective partnerships.

Cultural Competence as an Organizing Principle

The study of organizational culture has become a major domain of institutional research...eclipsing studies of formal structure, organizational-environment, and of bureaucracy (Ouchi & Wilkins, 1985). William Tierney (1985) suggests that while understanding the organizational culture is not a panacea to all administrative problems, an administrator's accurate interpretation of the culture can provide critical insight about which options to choose in decision making. Schein (1985) defines culture "as a pattern of shared basic assumptions that the group learned as it solved its problems... that has worked well enough to be considered valid and, therefore, to be taught to new members as the correct way to perceive, think, and feel in relation to those problems" (p. 12). In short, culture is a set of shared values that governs behavior within organizations.

As institutions expand and grow, faculty become more specialized and faculty and staff receive different types of training, the appearance of subcultures within the organization increases. These subcultures hold different values, beliefs and communicate differently from one another. In order to successfully navigate this maze and effectively work across the siloes, individuals and subcultures within the organization can become culturally competent (OCCRL, 2014).

According to Cross, et. al (1989), cultural competence is a "set of congruent behaviors, attitudes, and policies that come together in a system, agency, or amongst professionals and enables that system, agency, or those professionals to work effectively in cross-cultural situations" (p. 7). The use of the term "competence" is contested because it suggests expertise or mastery in a particular area. Within the context of cultural competence, however, "competence" implies that an individual or system has the capacity to work effectively (Cross, et al, 1989). As such, there is always more to learn and comprehend about one's personal worldview as well as the worldview of others. Thus, cultural competence is a developmental process. There are no quick fixes, and there is no defined end.

Cultural Competence is a Developmental Process

The culture of individuals, systems, and organizations falls on a continuum, ranging from cultural destruction to cultural proficiency. There are countless possibilities between these extremes. Cross, et al (1989) identified the following six points on the continuum:

- Cultural destructive – Attitudes, policies and practices seek to destroy cultures that differ from the dominant culture. In an academic setting, academic faculty members may find themselves uninvolved in the work of the college beyond the classroom, due to a growing number of student services professionals.
- Cultural incapacity – Subtle attitudes and practices that make staff or faculty feel unwelcomed or unimportant
- Cultural blindness – Culture is unimportant, hence all staff and faculty are the same. This point on the continuum promotes cultural assimilation.
- Cultural pre-competence – Subcultures begin to assess and recognize their individual culture and how it interacts with other cultures. Weaknesses are exposed and the desire to interact with other subcultures emerges.
- Cultural competence – Acceptance and respect for diversity, continuing self-assessment, careful attention to inherent

dynamics when different cultures interact, an expanding institutional cultural knowledge and experimenting with a variety of adaptations.
- Cultural proficiency – A higher level of cultural competency. Culture is of high regard. Culture guides and drives decision-making.

The degree of cultural competence is a function of individual or organizational attitudes, policies, and practices. As an individual or organization makes adaptations to value and appreciate diversity, as well as build institutional cultural knowledge, growth in the positive direction occurs.

A culturally competent individual, group, system, or organization is identifiable by the following characteristics: a) values diversity, b) possesses the capacity for cultural self-assessment, c) is conscious of the dynamics inherent when cultures interact, d) possesses institutionalized cultural knowledge, and e) develops adaptations to diversity" (Cross, et al, 1989). The next section of this chapter will briefly discuss each tenet of cultural competency within the context of developing effective partnerships between academic and student affairs personnel.

Capacity for Self-Assessment

Self-assessment is necessary to help each functional area understand its culture. It is essential for student service personnel as well as academic administrators and faculty members to independently identify and understand how their particular culture will interact with other cultures. To enact self-assessment, each area must enter a period of self-reflection (OCCRL, 2014) and inter-group dialogue (Arcelus, 2011). Self-reflection might include such guiding questions as: Who are we/am I relative to the mission? What behaviors are rewarded in this area? What does this functional area contribute to the academic mission? How might our culture differ from other cultures? What skills, knowledge do we/I need to hear and be heard/work and work with others across cultures?

Valuing Diversity

There are different views on student learning and development within a community college. Most community colleges continue to divide interactions with students into two distinct functional units: academic affairs and student affairs. According to Arcelus (2011), the origins of this divide are the result of a longstanding debate about whether or not the undergraduate experience is about the mind or life of a student. Faculty members are the primary inhabitants of academic affairs. Faculty members own the curriculum and carry out the vast majority of instructional duties. On the other hand, student affairs professionals provide supports such as admissions and enrollment, recruitment, financial aid, tutoring, and counseling, among others. The exact portfolio of supports varies across community colleges (Cohen & Brawer, 2008). Contemporary perspectives on the divide suggest that campuses push against the false dichotomies in search of global and holistic experiences for students (Arcelus, 2011).

In this context, it is important for community college leaders to recognize and value the different contributions made by academic and student affairs makes toward student collaborative partnerships are "a culture in which all participants are viewed as equal partners who play equally important roles and have significant contributions to make" (p. 19). Acceptance of the different contribution (as opposed to valuation and ranking of the different contributions) made by each area can help the institution begin devising new ways of interacting with students. Efforts to resist the temptation to devalue student services in an academic enterprise are essential.

Conscious of Dynamics of Cultural Interaction

What happens during interactions between academicians and student affairs professionals interact? Due to differences in deeply held values and beliefs about student learning across functional area, academicians, and student affairs professionals do not always

understand each other (Arcelus, 2011). Personnel from each area are likely to bring to bear culturally prescribed patterns of communication, interaction, and problem solving as well as stereotypes and frustrations about working with "the other" to bear (Cross, et al, 1989). Cross-cultural interactions are naturally
tense due to misunderstandings, mistrust, disrespect, conflict, disdain, and antagonism. The energy created during these interactions is the consequence of two-way exchanges that violate cultural norms of another.

Being aware of the natural tensions, leaders are positioned to navigate towards an appreciation of differences, a search for similarities, and more effective partnerships between academic and student affairs units.

Institutionalize Cultural Knowledge

Addressing cultural issues is an arduous task. The various cultures that exist within an institution have differing and oftentimes conflicting views on efforts that influence student development (Shehane & Dewsnap, 2012).

Understandings of the various cultures that define an organization are foundational to the development of effective partnerships between academic and student affairs (Shehane & Dewsnap, 2012). Once members of an organization become self-aware of their individual cultures, dialogue is necessary to promote sharing across the cultural divide. The quest of the ensuing dialogue is to understand different cultures in relationship to each other as well as to understand how each culture views the mission and their role within that mission. Translation of this new knowledge from the dialogue must become institutional policy and practice to create an institutional ethos that supports effective partnerships.

Furthermore, the definition of partnership is likely to evolve from simply coming together to create a program or initiative, to a substantive search for mutual understanding, trust, and commitment to create an institutional ethos that supports holistic learning (Arcelus, 2011).

Adaptations to Diversity

Cook, Eaker, Gherling, and Sells (2007) define collaborative partnerships as "a culture in which all participants are viewed as equal partners who play equally important roles and have significant contributions to make" (p. 19). To develop partnerships between academic and student affairs, institutional leaders must cultivate synergistic relationships built on trust, mutual understanding, and commitment to share the vision and actions for student learning and development.

Exercises to Initiate Quest for Effective Partnership

Many college faculty and staff are interested in building these cross-functional collaborative practices. Yet, many of these interested faculty and staff are unsure about how to structure and facilitate the dialogue. The following activities may "jump" start institutional thinking about how to support dialogue as a lead in to establishing effective collaborations between academic and student affairs functional areas.

Assemble a group of individual staff from student affairs and faculty from various disciplines for a facilitated conversation. The expected outcomes of the interactive session below include helping participants be: (a) open to learning about themselves, their group's cultures as well as the culture of others on campus and (b) willing to engage in self and group reflection to improve cross-cultural skills in the work setting. The steps include:

- Introducing Yourself – Tell us something about yourself that connects to your familial culture or cultural background.
- Experiences with the Other – Identify and ask a volunteer to discuss how it feels moving between student affairs and academic affairs during their career.
- Searching for Similarities – What are your perceptions about academic affairs professional and student affairs professionals?

- Appreciative Inquiry About Effective Collaborations – Each person in the room should be invited to find someone in the room to pair with. The partners should not know each other well. Each partner should be given 15 minutes to interview each other. At the conclusion of the interview period, each pair will read each their partner's responses to the audience.
    - Describe a time that you were part of an effective team or partnership?
        - Looking at the entire experience, recall a time when you felt most alive, most involved, or most excited about your involvement.
        - What made the experience exciting?
        - Who was involved?
        - Describe the team and the work.
    - Without being modest, what do you value about yourself? What do you value about yourself at work?

Conclusion

This chapter explored the use of cultural competency as an important guiding principle in developing effective partnerships between student and academic affairs in the community college setting. Student learning happens inside and outside the classrooms. Many community college leaders seek ways to create holistic learning environments, where curricular and co-curricular efforts coalesce to support the overarching mission. Successful partnerships between academic affairs and student services are challenging. Differences in the development, evolution, and function create cultural and structural divisions between the two functional areas. The differences are at times difficult to bridge. Cultural competency provides a pathway to address the chasm.

References

American Association of Community Colleges (2015). *American Association of Community College fast fact sheet.* Retrieved from http://www.aacc.nche.edu/AboutCC/Pages/fastfactsfactsheet.aspx.

Arcelus, V.J. (2011). If student affairs-academic affairs collaboration is such a good idea, why are there so few examples of these partnerships in American higher education? P. Magolda & Marcia B. Baxter Mogolda (Eds.), Contested Issues in Student Affairs (pp. 61-74). Sterling, VA: Stylus.

Cohen, A. M. & Brawer, F. B. (2008). *The American community college.* San Francisco: Jossey-Bass.

Cook, J. H., Eaker, R.E., Gherling, A.M., and Sells D. K. (2007). Collaboration: Definitions and barriers. In J.H. Cook & C.A. Lewis (Eds.), *Student and Academic Affairs Collaboration: The Divine Comity* (17-31). Washington, DC: National Association of Student Personnel Administration.

Cross, T. L., Bazron, B. J., Dennis, K.W., & Isaacs, M.R. (1989). Towards a culturally competent system of care. Retrieved from http://files.eric.ed.gov/fulltext/ED330171.pdf.

Dougherty, K. J. (2001). *The contradictory college.* Albany, NY: State University of New York Press.

Frost, R.A., Storm, S. L., Downey, J., Schultz, D.D. & Holland, T.A. (2010). Enhancing student learning with academic and student affairs collaboration. *Community College Enterprise, 16,* 37-51.

McCabe, R. H. (2003). *Yes we can: A community college guide for developing America's underprepared.* Washington, DC: American Association of Community Colleges.

Nevarez, C. & Wood, J. L. (2010). *Community college leadership and administration.* New York: Peter Lang Publishing.

Office of Community College Research and Leadership (2014). Cultural competence in pathways to results. *Insights on equity and outcomes. Retrieved from* http://occrl.illinois.edu/wp-content/uploads/cultural-competence-brief.pdf.

Ouchi, W. G. & Wilkins, A. L. (1985). Organizational culture. *Annual Review of Sociology, 11,* 457-483.

Provasnik, S. & Planty, M. (2008). *Community colleges: Special supplement to the condition of education 2008.* Washington, DC: National Center for Education Statistics, Institute of Education Sciences, U.S. Department of Education.

Shehane, M.E. & Dewsnap, M.A. (2012). Student affairs partnering with academic affairs knowledge community: Developing partnerships to influence change. Retrieved from http://www.naspa.org/images/uploads/main/2012-NASPA-KC-Spring-Publication.pdf.

Tierney, W. G. (2010). Organizational culture in higher education: Defining the essentials. In M.C. Brown II (Ed.), *Organization and Governance in Higher Education,* (328-339). Boston, MA: Pearson.

Weimer. M. (2013). *Learner-centered teaching: Five key changes to practices.* San Francisco, CA: Jossey-Bass.

WestEd and the RP Group (2012). Question 6: Integrating academic and student affairs. Retrieved from http://www.wested.org/online_pubs/resource1245F.pdf.

Chapter Four

Multicultural Relationships within the Academic Setting: The Influence of Power and Cultural Trust

By Adriana Peña, RoShunna Lea, Catherine Burke, Virginia Frazier, & DeDe Wohlfarth

Our society has a long history of privileging selected demographic groups and disadvantaging others. Academic institutions, as stalwarts of society's status quo, replicate and exacerbate this problem (Evans & DeVita, 2016) by affording societal advantages to those who identify as White, Christian, cisgender, heterosexual, middle or upper-class, able-bodied men. Historically, women, people of color, and other lesser represented individuals were limited or excluded from entrance to academia and thus diversity among faculty appointments has suffered (National Center for Educational Statistics, 2016; HRSA, 2015; Fuhrmann, Halme, O'Sullivan, & Lindstaedt, 2011). Although marginalized groups are no longer formally barred from institutions of higher education, these individuals continue to endure both subtle and overt discrimination which perpetuates the downgrading of targeted populations (Evans & De Vita, 2016). To promote learning and growth for diverse students on campus, strategies are discussed to create an academic environment that fosters inclusivity and decreases animosity between different racial, cultural, and ethic members of the academic community.

As colleges and universities are tasked with diversity initiatives to increase the percentage of students and faculty from underrepresented minority (URM) populations (NIH, 2015), difficulties with retention and campus climate persist. To support students and faculty of color, and those who are from marginalized groups or cultures, institutions of learning must implement long-term strategies to change the academic culture. Simply categorically increasing enrollment numbers perpetuates the historic underachievement and high drop-out rates found in minority students (Irving & Hudley, 2005). Cultural knowledge and humility are critical to successful strategies to cultivate an inclusive environment by addressing institutional power differentials, stereotype threat, and campus climates (Allen, Scott, & Lewis, 2013).

Campus Diversity Initiatives

As colleges and universities are tasked with diversity initiatives to increase the percentage of students and faculty from underrepresented minority (URM) populations (NIH, 2015), difficulties with retention and campus climate persist. To support students and faculty of color, and those who are from marginalized groups or cultures, institutions of learning must implement long-term strategies to change the academic culture. Simply categorically increasing enrollment numbers perpetuates the historic underachievement and high drop-out rates found in minority students (Irving & Hudley, 2005). Cultural knowledge and humility are critical to successful strategies to cultivate an inclusive environment by addressing institutional power differentials, stereotype threat, and campus climates (Allen, Scott, & Lewis, 2013).

The demographics and political climate of the United States have shifted over the past few decades, creating a need for academic institutions to recognize how changes in our universities mirror our larger communities (Allen, Scott & Lewis, 2013). The era of civil rights and 2003 upholding of Affirmative Action by the Supreme Court (Gratz v. Bollinger, n.d.) increased the validity and institutional benefits of diverse learning environment. U.S. policy makers reinforced this focus with the availability of grant funding for those from URM backgrounds in following years (NIH, 2015). An eruption of diversity initiatives and allocated funds at academic institutions developed to better replicate the racial and cultural diversity of the country, with a specific goal of attracting and retaining minority students. However, the success of such initiatives widely varied. When the sole focus of diversity initiatives becomes increasing the underrepresented demographic groups on campus, the positive benefits of exposure to diversity loses its value.

In general, as the number of URM students increased on a campus, so, too, did the range of opinions and values within these racial groups (Chang, Milem, & Antonio, 2011). The goal of diversity efforts should be to expose all students to an increasingly broad range of values, beliefs, and opinions regarding a range of social and political issues. For example, students should be exposed to others who think differently than they do about healthcare, capital punishment, politics, and the prevalence of discrimination (Chang, Milem, & Antonio, 2011). To expose students to a wide range of views, even the voice of a single minority person must be supported. Unfortunately, without adequate faculty and administrative preparation (Gay, 2002), this support is uncommon. Instead, the educational system tends to solidify current barriers that contribute to systemic oppression.

The wide-reaching effects of the adversity and discrimination experienced by members of marginalized groups in and outside of academia is well documented (CCCC, 2013; Green, 2016). These experiences are compounded by microaggressions from peers and faculty, as well as teaching/ learning objectives rooted in Western ideals (Hain-Jamall, 2013; Sue, 2015). The negative effects of discrimination and racism have been well documented, and include physical, mental, social, economic, and political marginalization (Penner, Blair, Albrecht, & Dovidio, 2014; Berger & Sarnyai, 2015). Among Hispanic Americans, Asian Americans, and African Americans, discrimination has been shown to increase the level of psychological disorders (Chou, Asnaani, & Hofmann, 2012). Additionally, the development of trauma symptomology may result (Bryant-Davis & Ocampo, 2006; Cheng & Mallinckrodt, 2015). Experiences of racism may be particularly salient during the formidable years of college as students are developing and strengthening their identities (Gurin et al., 2002). Because of these experiences, students from marginalized groups may show an understandable mistrust of authority.

Power and Authority within Institutions. The constructs of power and trust are crucial to understanding negative stereotypes, bias, "-isms," microaggressions, discrimination, and institutional racism. To truly promote inclusivity, fairness, and social justice, and to achieve meaningful multicultural relationships, requires honestly examining the role of power in academia. An environment that is truly respectful for all students requires nimble management by administrators and faculty to balance factors that influence control and trust at the macro and micro level. This critical, and exceedingly difficult, task is necessary to move beyond superficial representations of appearing "tolerant" and "accepting" of differences.

The *Culture of Academic Power.* In the late 1980s, Delpit (1988) explored the role of power in higher education. Delpit suggested that students be explicitly taught to navigate the power structures in academia to increase the likelihood for positive adjustment and retention. Delpit (1988) noted that societal power is re-enacted in classroom as a microcosm of society. Rules exist within our classrooms to maintain our current hierarchy, a distribution of power that he called the "culture of power." Majority culture individuals establish this culture without respect or consideration of marginalized individuals. The majority cultural group values and standards are implicitly recognized as the mainstream or appropriate ones, a process which facilitates and simplifies group or classroom membership for most individuals. Like societal power structures, once the classroom microcosm is established, the most powerful members are least cognizant of the created disparities (Delpit, 1988).

Delpit (1988) recommends that students outside the dominant culture be explicitly taught how this culture of power permeates the classroom. Students from middle and upper-socio economic status backgrounds understand these implicit rules, and thus have an advantage over others (Delpit, 1988). For example, if a person is charged with a crime and experiences his first court hearing, he is likely to experience less anxiety if he is educated on proper attire, courtroom procedure, and his expected participation. Likewise, if a person moves to a remote Alaskan village, her adjustment would be facilitated by a native of the village sharing information about local dress and social customs (Delpit, 1988). By extension of this idea, effective mentoring of minority students provides explicit directions for succeeding in academia. Effective mentoring also validates and values the student's culture and identity.

Paternalism. Further contributing to the difficulties of URM students on campus is *paternalism*, where an individual in a societal position of power appears helpful and benevolent but is actually engaging in behaviors that are condescending or patronizing (Jackman, 1994 as cited by McCoy, Winkle-Wagner, & Luedke, 2015). These authors found rampant White paternalism on college campuses, as White faculty members often believed that students of color were "academically underprepared," and needed to be brought "up to speed." The occurrence of White paternalism is a re-enactment of power hierarchy described by Delpit (1988).

Cultural Mistrust

Students from marginalized groups are also likely to harbor cultural mistrust caused by generations of systemic oppression and personal experiences with such oppression. Students from minority populations often report a lack of support on their academic campus (Green, 2016). Students of color specifically report feeling overwhelmingly disconnected from their white peers and faculty, perceive that the campus cannot meet their expectations, and their campus exacerbates the effects of societal oppression (Green, 2016).

The political attacks on specific marginalized groups during and after the election for the 45th president of the United States resulted in high national tensions, including college campuses (DeVega, 2017; Sutton, 2017). According to the Southern Poverty Law Center (SPLC, 2016), 867 reports of intimidation and harassment were made in the ten days after Donald J. Trump was elected. This statistic is particularly alarming because according to SPLC (2016), the Bureau of Justice reports that two-thirds of hate crimes go unreported. Approximately 16% (140) of the 867 reported incidents occurred at universities (SPLC, 2016). Thousands of anecdotal reports by teachers were made to Teaching Tolerance during this same time frame, creating legitimate concerns about post-election safety on college campuses (Magee, 2017).

These events resulted in greater distrust among cultural and religious groups, as well as an increase in political activity and intensified racial and cultural conversations on campus (Ojalvo, 2017). This intensification is most likely a positive step, provided educators and students have the resources and skills to navigate the difficult climate. The real danger is that efforts to increase diversity on campuses may be overshadowed by incidents of campus racism and discrimination (Kineavy, 2016). Many forms of racism, and its effects, may be overlooked (Carter, 2007; Helms, Nicolas, & Green, 2012).Minority subcultures have historic justification to distrust members of the majority culture due to violent persecution, oppression, and discrimination. This understandable mistrust, or healthy cultural paranoia, serves a self-protective role for individuals (Ridley, 1984; Ridley, 1986). Although healthy cultural paranoia may serve a protective function, research has demonstrated a negative outcome on such cultural mistrust for students of color in higher education (Ridley, 1984; Ridley, 1986). When students mistrust their faculty members, such mistrust contributes to academic dis-identification, including lower levels of engagement and learning (McCain & Cokley, 2017). This dis-identification increase the chances of dropping out of school. Additionally, higher levels of cultural mistrust may result in decreased self-esteem, lower academic expectations, and poorer academic outcomes (Irving & Hudley, 2005) The biggest contributors to cultural mistrust include institutional racism, systemic inequities, microaggressions, unresolved power differential issues, lack of effective mentoring, and "colorblind" others (CCCC, 2013; Sue, 2015).

The experience of stereotype threat, or the fear of conforming to expected notions of a stereotyped group, explains how these experiences disenfranchise students from academia. Irving and Hudley (2005) recommend that educators work to understand the reasons for a student's cultural mistrust so as to work through these barriers with students. Similarly, faculty and staff are not immune from cultural mistrust, and interpersonal relationships throughout an institution can thus affect the overall campus climate (Green, 2016). As educators better understand the impact of cultural mistrust, we will be better prepared to develop strategies that establish safety, interconnectedness, and harmony.

Intimacy, Trust, and Control

Teacher-student relationships are built on three central dimensions: intimacy, trust, and control (Dobransky & Framier, 2004). Each teacher-student relationship has tugs and pulls towards the different dimensions, depending on numerous factors, including the demands and needs of individuals within the relationship. Students who develop closeness, trust, and a sense of shared control with their professors reported higher levels of learning in their classes (Dobransky & Framier, 2004). Communication outside of the classroom, such as advisor- advisee and mentoring relationships are particularly helpful at facilitating intimacy and shared control. A key to develop personal and authentic relationships with students without violating boundaries or blurring roles (Dobransky & Framier, 2004). These supportive relationships are particularly important for students of color (Cole & Griffin, 2013).

Cultural Humility

The lack of cultural competence is not due to a deficiency in knowledge, as is commonly believed, but rather self-awareness and attitudes (Tervalon & Murray-Garcia, 1998). Cultural humility has been suggested as an important goal in education, beyond cultural competence (Tervalon & Murray-Garcia, 1998). Cultural humility emphasizes lifelong learning instead of the mastery of a finite body of knowledge implied by the term cultural competence. This journey involves using self-reflection, checking power imbalances, and developing non-paternalistic dialogue. The paradigm change is to recognize that no one can ever be fully "culturally competent." True cultural competence would require not only an encyclopedic knowledge of all cultures in the world, but a knowledge of each subculture as well. The truly culturally competent individual also would need to demonstrate the skills to work with individuals from numerous cultures. Finally, a culturally competent person would need an inexhaustible ability to mindfully self-reflect, to ascertain his or her biases, prejudices, or stereotypes were managed in the context of a relationship with any culturally diverse other.

Since cultures are constantly changing, skill sets evolving, and attitudes in flux, no one can every truly become culturally competent, although this should not discourage us from seeking such a goal. The awareness that one can never finish a goal but is willing to work towards it despite such ambiguity is a critical attitude towards cultural humility. We must stay committed to being lifelong learners and understand that we will never know what to do or say in every situation (Gallardo, 2014). As such, our commitment should be towards continue collaboration and increasing appreciation for each person's unique culture and background. Cultural humility acknowledges that people will make mistakes, and that growing from these mistakes is vital to moving forward.

Models to Explore

To promote learning and growth for all students on campus, faculty will need to meaningfully advance diversity (Chang, Milem, & Antonio, 2011). Working with students from a wide variety of backgrounds will require both flexibility and humility on behalf of educators.

Culturally Responsive Teaching. Gay (2002; 2010) defined culturally responsive teaching as "using the cultural characteristics, experiences, and perspectives of ethnically diverse students as conduits for teaching them more effectively" (p. 106). Academic skills are learned more easily if those lessons are meaningful and relevant to one's own frame of reference (Gay,2010). Additionally, students from the nondominant cultures have unique cultural experiences and knowledge which can improve the learning environment for all students (Bernal, 2002; Yosso, 2005). Thus, faculty member must make multiple efforts to reach out to students of color, and to ensure that classroom material connect with them through examples, cultural values, stories, and real-life problem based assignments. Gay (2010) delineated five essential elements for culturally responsive teaching. These include the development of a strong knowledge regarding cultural diversity, inclusion of culture- based content within the course curriculum, the development of learning communities, open communication with ethnically diverse students, and appropriate responses to ethnic diversity. As is true for our work to become culturally humble, becoming culturally responsive educators is a lifelong journey with no clear endpoint.

Sanctuary model. Educators must vigilantly work to develop policies and procedures to effectively manage discriminatory incidents and maintain safety, a process epitomized by the sanctuary model. Creating a campus to become a sanctuary from all forms of "isms" means becoming more respectful and inclusive of all individuals (Bloom & Sreedhar, 2008). According to the New York Times, 28 campuses have declared themselves as sanctuary campuses in response to anti-immigration policies, providing a safe haven for all individuals (Preston, 2017). Although the decision to become a sanctuary campus is a university wide process, faculty can nevertheless take steps to consider how to create classroom sanctuaries.

Faculty Mentoring

Faculty mentoring is critical to the academic success of minority undergraduate (Quaye & Harper, 2014) and graduate students (Hollingsworth & Fassinger, 2002). However, while faculty mentoring has strong potential to help students of color succeed, it also may reinforce racial and structural inequities (McCoy,

2015). McCoy (2015) notes White faculty often take a colorblind approach with students, and attempt to treat non-White and White students the same. While this approach may seem to be rooted in fairness, it does not change the status quo of institutional racism.

Bonilla-Silva (2010) described several types of colorblindness which may be taken by white faculty simultaneously: abstract liberalism, naturalization, cultural racism, and minimization of racism. These colorblind approaches dismiss student's racial, ethnic, and cultural identities (McCoy, Winkle-Wagner, & Luedke, 2015), and ignore the cultural wealth students of color (Yosso, 2005). According to McCoy, Winkle-Wagner, & Luedke (2015), many White faculty believe that students of color should "assimilate" and "leave part of themselves at the school house door." (p. 237). However, a more helpful approach is for faculty to be aware of their students' multiple identities, and to work to understand these identities.

One key to understanding students' identities is to truly understand the reasons students are pursing college or graduate level degrees. Most graduate students cite similar reasons for seeking an advanced degree, including a desire to teach, expand their knowledge, and conduct research (Brunsma, Embrick & Shin, 2017). Women and minority students, however, provide different primary reasons for seeking a degree, commonly citing the power of education to benefit one's own community (Brunsma, Embrick & Shin, 2017). Faculty members can help students of color by talking openly about the reasons they are pursuing educational degrees. These conversations can help defuse identity tension, which diverse students may feel as the academic environment pressures them to abandon their cultural identities, while also addressing the pressure from within their cultures to maintain their cultural identity (Green, 2016).

When mentoring minority students, several factors are vital to success (Alvarez, Blume, Cervantes, & Thomas, 2009). These factors include supporting the student's attempt to navigate multiple worlds (i.e. career, cultural, familial, and academic), increasing awareness of power and authority, clarifying the expectations of academia, providing education about cultural diversity, having discussions about multiple identities that may conflict with one another, acknowledging the existence of discrimination inside and outside of the academic setting, and teaching coping skills to manage future experiences of discrimination.

Conclusion

To maximize the educations of students of color, instructors must be open, caring, and flexible to adjust to the varying needs and contexts of their students (McAllister, 2002). Educators must be aware of and support students' differences, although this idea is in direct opposition to the colorblind approach many advocated historically (McCoy, Winkle-Wagner, & Luedke, 2015). By teaching in a culturally responsive way, dealing forthrightly with issues of control, working to gain trust despite cultural mistrust, and mentoring students of color; faculty members can create campuses in which all students can maximize their learning. Essential to such learning is to ensure students of color feel validated, heard, and appreciated, as well as feeling safe from racism and discrimination that continue to pervade our society.

Acknowledging systemic and educational biases and power differentials are crucial to developing trusting relationships. To acknowledge, understand, and appropriately express empathy about these systemic problems requires knowledge about other cultures, but more importantly, a degree of cultural humility. Interwoven throughout these efforts must be the values of respect and cultural responsibility (Kumar, Karabenick, & Burgoon, 2015).

The benefits of creating a more accepting and inclusive environment are far reaching. By continuing to advocate for social justice and equality, we begin to erode some of the societal structures that have allowed institutional racism to flourish. Finally, by developing ways to value, appreciate, and respect the cultural wealth of diverse individuals, institutions can create optimal learning environments which benefit the entire academic community (Gurin et al.,2002). Acknowledging systemic and educational biases and power differentials are crucial to developing trusting relationships. To acknowledge, understand, and appropriately express empathy about these systemic problems requires knowledge about other cultures, but more importantly, a degree of cultural humility. Interwoven throughout these efforts must be the values of respect and cultural responsibility (Kumar, Karabenick, & Burgoon, 2015). The benefits of creating a more accepting and inclusive environment are far reaching. By continuing to advocate for social justice and equality, we begin to erode some of the societal structures that have allowed institutional racism to flourish. Finally, by developing ways to value, appreciate, and respect the cultural wealth of diverse individuals, institutions can create optimal learning environments which benefit the entire academic community (Gurin et al.,2002).

References

Allen, A., Scott, L. M., & Lewis, C. W. (2013). Racial microaggressions and African American and Hispanic Students in urban schools: A call for culturally affirming education. *Interdisciplinary Journal of Teaching and Learning, 3*(2), 117-129.

Alvarez, A. N., Blume, A. W., Cervantes, J. M., & Thomas, L. R. (2009). Tapping the wisdom tradition: Essential elements to mentoring students of color. *Professional Psychology: Research and Practice, 40*(2), 181.

Berger, M., & Sarnyai, Z. (2015). 'More than skin deep': Stress neurobiology and mental health consequences of racial discrimination. *Stress: The International Journal on the Biology of Stress, 18*(1), 1-10. doi:10.3109/10253890.2014.989204.

Bernal, D. D. (2002). Critical race theory, Latino critical theory, and critical raced-gendered epistemologies: Recognizing students of color as holders and creators of knowledge. *Qualitative inquiry, 8*(1), 105-126.

Bloom, S. L., & Sreedhar, S. Y. (2008). The sanctuary model of trauma-informed organizational change. *Reclaiming children and youth, 17*(3), 48.

Bonilla-Silva, E. (2010). Racism without racist: Colorblind racism and racial inequality in Contemporary America (3rd ed.). Lanham, MD: Rowman & Littlefield.

Brunsma, D. L., Embrick, D. G., & Shin, J.H. (2017). Graduate students of color: Race, racism, and mentoring in the White waters of academia. *Sociology of Race and Ethnicity, 3(1),* 1-13.

Bryant-Davis, T., & Ocampo, C. (2006). A therapeutic approach to the treatment of racist-incident-based trauma. *Journal of Emotional Abuse, 6*(4), 1-22. doi:10.1300/J135v06n04_0.

California Community College Collaborative (CCCC). (2013, July). *Community colleges and their faculty of color: Matching teachers and students (A report to the*

Community Colleges of California). Retrieved from http://c4.ucr. edu/documents/ GSP2report_C4finalJuly152013.pdf.

Carter, R. T. (2007). Racism and Psychological and Emotional Injury: Recognizing and Assessing Race-Based Traumatic Stress. *Counseling Psychologist, 35*(1), 13-105.

Chang, M. J., Milem, J. F., & Antonio, A. L. (2011). Campus climate and diversity. *Student services: A handbook for the profession*, 43-58.

Cheng, H.-L., & Mallinckrodt, B. (2015). Racial/ethnic discrimination, posttraumatic stress symptoms, and alcohol problems in a longitudinal study of Hispanic/Latino college students. *Journal of Counseling Psychology, 62*(1), 38-49.

Chou, T, Asnaani, A. & Hofmann, S. (2012). Perception of Racial Discrimination and Psychopathology Across Three U.S. Ethnic Minority Groups. *Cultural Diversity & Ethnic Minority Psychology, 18*(1), 74-81.

Cole, D., & Griffin, K. A. (2013). Advancing the study of student-faculty interaction: A focus on diverse students and faculty. In *Higher education: Handbook of theory and research* (pp.561-611). Springer Netherlands.

Delpit, L. (1988). The silenced dialogue: Power and pedagogy in educating other people's children. *Harvard Educational Review, 58*(3), 280-299.

DeVega, C. (2017, March 8). Trump's election has created "safe spaces" for racists: Southern Poverty Law Center's Heidi Beirich on the wave of hate crimes. Retrieved from http://www.salon.com/2017/03/08/trumps-election-has-created-safe-spaces-for-racists- southern-poverty-law-centers-heidi-beirich-on-the-wave-of-hate-crimes/.

Dobransky, N. D., & Frymier, A. B. (2004). Developing teacher - student relationships through out of class communication. *Communication Quarterly, 52*(3), 211-223.

Evans, N. J., & DeVita, J. (2016). Diversity in Higher Education. *Student Affairs for Academic Administrators*, 33.

Fuhrmann, C. N., Halme, D. G., O'Sullivan, P. S., & Lindstaedt, B. (2011). Improving graduate education to support a branching career pipeline: Recommendations based on a survey of doctoral students in the basic biomedical sciences. *Life Sciences Education*, 10, 239-249.

Gallardo, M.E. (2014). *Developing cultural humility: Embracing race, privilege, and power.* Thousand Oaks, CA: Sage Publications, Inc.

Gay, G. (2002). Preparing for culturally responsive teaching. *Journal of Teacher Education, 53*(2), 106-116.

Gay, G. (2010). *Culturally responsive teaching: Theory, research, and practice.* Teachers College Press.

Gratz v. Bollinger. (n.d.) *Oyez.* Retrieved 2017 Feb 26, from https://www.oyez.org/cases/2002/02-516

Green, A. (2016, Jan 21). The cost of balancing academia and racism. Retrieved from https://www.theatlantic.com/education/archive/2016/01/balancing-academia-racism/424887/.

Gurin, P., Dey, E., Hurtado, S., & Gurin, G. (2002). Diversity and higher education:

Theory and impact on educational outcomes. *Harvard Educational Review*, *72*(3), 330-367.

Hain-Jamall, D.A.S. (2013). Native-American & Euro-American cultures: comparative look at the intersection between language and worldview. *Multicultural Education*, *21*(1), 13-19.

Helms, J., Nicolas, G., & Green, C. (2012). Racism and ethnoviolence as trauma: Enhancing professional training. *Traumatology, 16*(4), 53-62.

Hollingsworth, M. A., & Fassinger, R. E. (2002). The role of faculty mentors in the research training of counseling psychology doctoral students. *Journal of Counseling Psychology*,*49*(3), 324.

Irving, M. A., & Hudley, C. (2005). Cultural mistrust, academic outcome expectations, and outcome values among African American adolescent men. *Urban Education*, *40*(5), 476-496.

Kineavy, F. (2016, September 26). Racist Incidents on College Campuses Cloud New School Year. Retrieved March 12, 2017, from http://www.diversityinc.com/news/racist-incidents-college-campuses-cloud-new-school-year/

Kumar, R., Karabenick, S. A., & Burgoon, J. N. (2015). Teachers' implicit attitudes, explicit beliefs, and the mediating role of respect and cultural responsibility on mastery and performance-focused instructional practices. *Journal of Educational Psychology*, *107*(2), 533.

Magee, M. (2017, January 08). Schools worry about campus tone in Trump era. Retrieved March 12, 2017, from http://www.sandiegouniontribune.com/news/education/sd-me-school-climate-20170105-story.html.

McAllister, G., & Irvine, J. J. (2002). The role of empathy in teaching culturally diverse students: A qualitative study of teachers' beliefs. *Journal of Teacher Education*, *53*(5), 433-443.

McClain, S., & Cokley, K. (2017). Academic dis-identification in Black college students: The role of teacher trust and gender. *Cultural Diversity and Ethnic Minority Psychology*, *23*(1), 125.

McCoy, D. L., Winkle-Wagner, R., & Luedke, C. L. (2015). Colorblind mentoring? Exploring white faculty mentoring of students of color. *Journal of Diversity in Higher Education*, *8*(4), 225.

National Center for Education Statistics (2016). Status and trends in the Education of racial and ethnic groups 2016. United States Department of Education. Available: https://nces.ed.gov/pubs2016/2016007.pdf . Accessed 2017 Feb 26.

National Institute of Health (2015). Evaluating the recruitment and retention plan to enhance diversity on T32 applications. Available: https://www.nigms.nih.gov/training/diversity/Pages/ReviewerInstructions.aspx . Accessed 2017 Feb 26National Institute of Health (2015). Notice of the NIH's interest in Diversity. Available: https://grants.nih.gov/grants/guide/notice-files/NOT-OD-15-053.html . Accessed 2017 Feb 26.

Ojalvo, H.E. (2017 January 20). Students protest Trump's inaugural on Campuses nationwide. Retrieved from http://college.usatoday.com/2017/01/20/students-are-protesting-trumps-inaugural-on-campuses-nationwide/.

Penner, L. A., Blair, I. V., Albrecht, T. L., & Dovidio, J. F. (2014). Reducing Racial Health

Care Disparities: A Social Psychological Analysis. *Health and Well-Being: Policy Insights from the Behavioral and Brain Sciences, 1*(1) 204–212.

Preston, J. (2017, January 26). Campuses Wary of Offering 'Sanctuary' to Undocumented Students. Retrieved March 12, 2017, from https://www.nytimes.com/2017/01/26/education/edlife/sanctuary-for-undocumented-students.html?_r=0.

Quaye, S. J., & Harper, S. R. (2014). *Student engagement in higher education: Theoretical perspectives and practical approaches for diverse populations*. Routledge.

Ridley, C. R. (1984). Clinical treatment of the nondisclosing Black client: A therapeutic paradox. *American Psychologist, 39*(11), 1234.

Ridley, C. R. (1986). Optimum service delivery to the Black client. *American Psychologist, 41*(2), 226-227.

Southern Poverty Law Center. (2016, November 29). Ten Days After: Harassment and Intimidation in the Aftermath of the Election. Retrieved March 12, 2017, from https://www.splcenter.org/20161129/ten-days-after-harassment-and- intimidation -aftermath-election.

Sue, D.W. (2015). *Race talk and the conspiracy of silence*. Hoboken, NJ: John Wiley & Sons.

Sutton, H. (2017). FBI releases report on increased hate crimes. *Campus Security Report, 13*(9), 9-9.

Tervalon, M., & Murray-Garcia, J. (1998). Cultural humility versus cultural competence: a critical distinction in defining physician training outcomes in multicultural education. *Journal of Health Care for the Poor and Underserved, 9*(2), 117-125.

Yosso, T. J. (2005). Whose culture has capital? A critical race theory discussion of community cultural wealth. *Race, Ethnicity and Education, 8*, 69–91. Retrieved from http://dx.doi.org/10.1080/1361332052000341006.

Chapter Five

Bridging the Digital Divide by Decreasing the Power Differential in Online and Hybrid Classrooms

By Michael Daniel, Mackenzie Hoffman, & DeDe Wohlfarth

Education is consistently evolving and with the exponential growth of online classrooms, ensuring all students' needs are met across platforms is critical to promote optimal learning experiences. These adaptations are especially important when teaching diverse classrooms, as educators are not only modifying classrooms to digital formats but are often teaching to student with varying degrees of familiarity of and access to technology. To address these concerns, educators should be aware of their own cultural backgrounds, educational expectations, best practice pedagogy, and students' needs prior to designing on-line courses.

Everything in education relates to culture. Consider that culture influences how we acquire knowledge, transmit knowledge, and the inventions and innovations that transform education. Thus, no educational system, and indeed, no classroom, can be culture-free (Erickson, 2001). One powerful cultural influence on education is the rapid growth of online and hybrid classes. Indeed, the advent of the digital age has spawned three distinct formats for education: face-to-face, online, and hybrid (Benton, 2009; Patel, 2014). Face-to-face classrooms consist of the traditional classroom in which students learn in a physical classroom. On-line classrooms consist of learning solely online (e.g. via online videos, discussion board, and links to articles and websites). Hybrid classrooms combine aspects of both face-to-face and online classrooms (e.g. learning in the classroom and sharing videos through a learning management system).

Despite the rapid technological changes in our classrooms, researchers have only begun to consider how culture affects online classes. Are students of color enrolling in online classes? When they do, are the learning outcomes similar to White students? Do students of color have better learning outcomes when professors provide certain structures or supports? This chapter will explore these questions and provide some concrete recommendations that professors can adopt to ensure that students of color are not lost in this dramatic pedagogical transition. The challenges of people of color accessing technology, and the resulting disparity in terms of users of this technology has been called the digital divide (Braverman, 2016). This term will be used throughout this chapter to communicate these discrepancies, which one could understand as a form of technological racism.

Demographics of the Digital Divide

As a starting point for these questions, consider the impact of culture on the demographics of our classrooms, including marked shifts in the racial and ethnic composition of our classrooms over the past 40 years. In the academic year 1976-1977, a full 90% of students who received bachelor degrees from post-secondary institutions were White, with only 10% of all bachelor's level graduates representing people of color (U.S. Department of Education, 2016). This data contrasts strongly with data from the 2014-2015 academic year. In that year, the following percentages of students received bachelor degrees from post-secondary institutions: 67% White students, 12% Hispanic students, 11% Black students, 7% Asian/Pacific Islander students, 0.6% American Indian/Alaskan students, and 3.0% multiracial students (U.S. Department of Education, 2016). In comparing these numbers, a striking trend is apparent: our classrooms are becoming less White and more culturally diverse. In order to provide the best possible education to all students, professors need to ensure that our pedagogical approaches are thus culturally competent (Nolan, 2016).

With the move towards online classes, demographics have also drastically changed. Consider how different these demographics for on-line classes in 2011-2012 compare to some of the statistics referenced above. In this year, students whose degree program was entirely online consisted of the following demographic make-up: Black 9%, White 7%, American Indian/Alaskan Native, 7%, Two or More Races, 6%, Hispanic, 4%, Asian 3%, Pacific Islander, 3% (U.S. Department of Education, 2014). If overall numbers are considered, most students who are enrolled in online courses are White students. However, a notable proportion of minority students are enrolled in online courses. The percentage of students of color in on-line classes is likely to continue to grow, as students continue to weigh the benefits of on-line learning, including convenience, cost, and the potential for a more diverse culture of learners (Kumar, 2015).

Despite these increasing numbers of students of color in on-line classes, the digital divide remains a barrier for many students. In the United States, the country as a whole is quick to adopt information and communication technologies (Ayanso, Cho, & Lertwachara, 2014; Braverman, 2016). However, this spread of technology is not uniform. Technology frequently begins in more affluent regions of the country and slowly moves toward communities of lower socioeconomic status (Ayanso, Cho, & Lertwachara, 2014; Braverman, 2016). Thus, students of color, who are disproportionately represented among lower income groups, are more likely to have less access to technological knowledge and resources. With the slow speed of technology dispersal and the rapidly changing landscape of the technology field, the digital divide that already exists has the potential to grow even wider, even within a country quick to embrace new technologies.

Students who can easily afford to their basic needs (e.g. food, shelter) will seek out more self-actualizing activities and have more opportunity to learn how to benefit from the internet or personal computers (Dewan & Riggins, 2005). Meanwhile, students whose basic needs are not met will likely not have access to a personal computer or internet capabilities, as these needs are a lower priority. Additionally, some students in rural settings may have limited access to secure and consistent internet (Stočes, Masner, & Jarolímek, 2015). In combination, these factors work to reduce the number of students of color in our online classes. Thus, one reason that professors need to be adopt more culturally competent practices in our teaching is to work to ensure more fair access to on-line classes in the first place.

Beyond Demographics: Social Capita and Resources

When students of color do enroll in online classes, access does not cease to be a problem for them. Many students who are financially strapped will have less access to a personal computer, laptop, internet capacities, and free wi-fi (Dewan & Riggins, 2005). In some instances, students may need to travel to a public library or other location to participate in online activities or to complete homework (Stočes, Masner, & Jarolímek, 2015). This added inconvenience can make online learning unnecessarily difficult for some students. Most commonly, students may lack adequate technology to access digital resources or participate in online discussions (Ayanso, Cho, & Lertwachara, 2014; Braverman, 2016).

As a concrete example of this problem, I share a story of one African American student who took a completely online course from me several years ago. This student was a single parent with three young children under six years of age. When I designed the course, I thought I had thoughtfully considered the individual needs of students. Therefore, students had a large window (48 hours) to complete their on-line exams. Moreover, students could retake parallel versions of exams if they were unhappy with their first scores. I thought this arrangement would encourage students who were performing poorly to work harder to master the material. I also believed that the 48-hour window to take an exam would take into account varying student schedules, including the needs of students working full time.

I noticed that one student was consistently performing far below her peers on her exams, scoring at the low D grade level at best. I reached out to her to better understand why, and decided to do so not only via an email, but through a phone call. During the phone call, I learned that this student, the aforementioned African American single parent, had no access to the internet except on Sunday nights from 6-8PM, when her church provided free computers and internet to church members. Unfortunately, child care was not provided. Every Sunday night, this student would take her three young children to the church basement and try to watch them as she completed the on-line exam. She had no time to try the exam a second time if her score was low, as the two-hour window of the church's open door policy did not allow enough time to finish two exams. Consider how poorly I had planned the class for this student, when I thought I had taken into account situational factors which might affect learning.

Sadly, I could give additional examples of my poor consideration of access to technology once students enrolled in my online classes. Perhaps the most humbling one was my belief that students had access to personal computers and laptops, for indeed our university library provides free desktops and laptops to students whenever it is open. Although this policy sounds generous, it does not help online learners who live far from campus, cannot easily travel, or students who work full-time and on weekends and have difficulty accessing the campus library. When I was giving feedback on an absolutely abysmal paper for class, I couldn't begin to understand why the formal research paper had so many formatting, typographical, grammatical, structural and organizational problems, until I learned that the student had typed the entire 5-page paper on her cell phone using google docs.

Examples such as these have served as powerful and humbling learning moments for me. They also have helped me think more carefully about the design of my online classes. In fact, the research supports that thoughtfully considering the individual needs of learners is one of the best ways we can design our on-line classes (Dole, Bloom, & Kowalske, 2016). Within the digital classroom, awareness of cultural differences and individual student needs are essential, especially when direct teacher-student interaction is lessened or not a component of the class. In face-to-face classes, we might become aware instances when our class rules or organizational structure are not working for students of a particular gender, race, or ethnicity. In an on-line classroom, we have no chance for such corrective feedback because we may not know the racial make-up of our classroom unless students self-disclose this information or we create an open forum where we can discuss race and ethnicity and their relation to the class content.

One concrete suggestion to help manage access issues is to ensure that students know about local institutions, such as public libraries and community centers, that provide internet access for members of the community who may not have reliable access at home (Braverman, 2016). By sharing these resources, teachers can help students feel more comfortable in navigating the digital landscape. Similarly, advocating for programs like ConnectEd, a national push to provide secure, stable internet in all classrooms, can help provide students and classrooms with better services (Braverman, 2016).

In optimal online classrooms, teachers seek to connect with students based on their individual needs. Ideal on-line environments model their classes around learners (Dole, Bloom, & Kowalske, 2016) and consider the learning needs, preferences, schedules, competing demanding, multiple roles, technological resources, technological access and other situational factors of the learners (Cavanaugh & Jacquemin, 2015; Chen, & Chiou, 2014; Yurdugül & Menzi Çetin, 2015). To design effective online classes, professors must understand the culture and needs of students prior to creating the digital course. Doing so can help lead to increased student satisfaction and online participation (Dole, Bloom, & Kowalske, 2016). These factors are highly correlated with learning.

Another key to designing culturally competent online classes is to utilize learner-centered teaching, which is possible even in an online environment (Weimer, 2013). The key premises of learner centered teaching include: 1) reconsidering the role of the instructor; 2) reconsidering the function of course content; 3) changing the balance of power; 4) shifting the responsibility of learning; and 5) reconsidering the purposes of evaluation. By creating a learner-centered classroom in online environments, teachers can elicit stronger student autonomy and increased interest in the subject matter. Higher student levels of control and increased interest in the subject matter eventually lead to improved academic and professional growth (Ahmed, 2010; Dole, Bloom, & Kowalske, 2016). Designing an on-line course to be learner-centered is beyond the scope this chapter, but such learner-centered approaches can be particularly helpful in meeting the needs of diverse students.

Another significant challenge to students of color in online classes relates to the idea of social capital (Chen & Chiou, 2014). Social capital refers to how resources are shared among groups of people and how information frequently stays within majority groups. For example, affluent, urban White groups typically have access to more information than minority groups (Chen & Chiou, 2014). This disparity is the result of prior inequality brought about by racial segregation and is perpetuated by groups sharing within their own ethnic and racial groups.

Consider how social capital plays out in an online classroom to affect student learning. Because students are more likely to pair up with and reach out to students who are similar to themselves, or who they perceive to be similar to themselves, White students tend to reach out to White students to form study groups, share course resources, work with in small groups, discuss course material, or otherwise engage in the course material. Likewise, students of color are more likely to reach out to other students of colors. The problem with this approach is that is perpetuates the digital divide, in that the students who have access to resources share them only with similar others, who likely also have access to such resources. Students with limited access to resources, which primarily involve students of color, are kept in the dark.

To challenge the existing social capital in online classes, researchers have suggested several key ideas. For example, to reduce unequal distribution of social capital, educators can establish training modules centered on teaching skills related to technology (Ayanso, Cho, & Lertwachara, 2014).

Through training, students who may not feel as competent in online formats can begin gaining familiarity and comfort with online tools, leading to success in future classes. Additionally, teachers must follow through and be aware of how students share resources, usually able to be observed through analysis of student activity in a learning management system. For example, sharing resources online may appear convenient; however, such sharing may need to happen across racial and gender divides.

Paying attention to students' abilities to navigate online content is also critical (Ayanso, Cho, & Lertwachara, 2014; Braverman, 2016). As previously mentioned, the ability to access resources can be hindered by lack of prior knowledge or lack of access to the internet. In these instances, creating alternatives can be tremendously beneficial to students (Stočes, Masner, & Jarolímek, 2015). By giving students options (e.g. supplying digital and physical copies of handouts; posting videos online and offering screenings within the classroom), students may feel more comfortable in the classroom knowing they can learn through the medium that feels most natural.

Direct Conversations about Race in Online Classes

In order to become a culturally competent teacher, professors must make conscious decisions, and often changes, in the way we have always taught our classes. The research that has previously been summarized in this book clearly demonstrates that racial microaggressions, or the "subtle insults (verbal, nonverbal, and/or visual) directed toward people of color, often automatically or unconsciously," are committed daily (Solórzano, Ceja, Yosso,

2000, p. 60). Racial microaggressions are noticed by students, with 63% of students of color experiencing subtle biases in the last year, and 44% of students noting obvious biases (Boysen, 2012). The commonality of microaggressions and biases suggests that educators must reconsider our teaching practices. If not, some students in all types of classrooms, including face-to-face, online, and hybrid classes, will experience decreased motivation, academic performance and ultimately less learning, related to the depletion of cognitive functioning among individuals who experience contemporary expressions of prejudice (Salvatore & Shelton, 2007; Sue, et al., 2009).

The best way to stop microaggressions, of course, is to educate students about them on the very first day of class (Booker, 2016). In online classrooms, students' responses to posted microaggressions are informed by their experiences with microaggressions offline (Williams, Oliver, Aumer, & Meyers, 2016). In other words, students must be aware of what a microaggression is and have the courage to point it out when it happens in their daily life before they are likely to be successful with such behavior in an on-line class. Thus, creating an ongoing dialogue about race and culture can help create a caring, safe space that empowers students to have open discussions online (McComb, 2015).

Microaggressions, whether online or face to face, require a response on behalf of the educator. For example, on-line class discussions can sometimes become intense debates about current societal issues as the professor works to connect course content with relevant real-world issues. These discussion forums can sometimes create situations in which students, whether intentionally or unintentionally, stereotype groups of people, engage in microaggressive behavior, or at their worst, engage in blatant and openly racist behavior through their comments and posts. The perceived anonymity of forums in an online class, in addition to social norms of "trolling" and the perception of safety and distant from others in an online environment make such negative behavior happen far more regularly than they might in our face-to-face classes (Summerville, 2005).

To deal with online microaggressions, the key is a vocal and visible response. The professor should not wait for students to respond to the microaggression, but should instead quickly post to explain why what the student posted was a problem. Follow up conversations, both publicly and privately, about prejudices and biases are one of the most effective responses we have (Boysen, 2012). Educators should be open to examining how we ourselves are individual products of cultural conditioning and inherited biases. In other words, we have to be willing to admit our own biases. This type of personal examination can be conducted in an online classroom, by modeling truthfulness and openness to students by leading discussions about marginalized groups, creating an environment of open conversation in which racism, sexism, and other biases are acknowledged, and demonstrating a willingness to share biases and limitations with students (Sue et al., 2009). Importantly, creating such an open environment must be regarded as an ongoing, continual process throughout the entire online course.

In closing, Sue (2009) suggests some helpful questions educators may ask themselves in designing culturally validating classrooms. These questions have been modified to emphasize the most critical elements in online classes:

- *What is the demographic make-up of students enrolled in my online course(s)?*
- *What type of access do students have to participate in the online environment? What special considerations might I need to make to assignment due dates based on accessibility/means? Am I available to all students equally?*
- *How can I incorporate ongoing conversations about biases and prejudices in an online environment? What special considerations may I need to make to monitor conversations?*
- *How might I outline my responsibilities and beliefs as a race-conscious educator in my description of teaching philosophy or course assignments?*
- *Given classroom communication is not face-to-face, how*

might racial microaggressions take place? How can I process and be an active agent in combatting these instances and consequently promote productive conversations?
- *How might the content of my online instruction reflect cultural conditioning?*
- *How might the current climate of society impact students learning given the instant access to news via the internet?*
- *Am I understanding of how all of my students feel they learn best? Do I make available a fair amount of ways to learn that works for all of my students?*
- *Do I seek regular student feedback and use that information to understand the climate of learning and instruction and/or implement changes if necessary?*

The following questions include important, overall personal reflections:
- *What are some of my biases or prejudices about different groups? When and how did I develop these beliefs? Am I open to challenging them?*
- *What are my privileges? How might this impact my ability to perceive perspectives from students of marginalized groups?*
- *What is my comfort level in facilitating ongoing conversations in various topics about biases and prejudices? What is my comfort level with challenging students' microaggressions, prejudices, or racism?*

By asking ourselves these tough questions, working to change the social capital in classrooms, sharing technological resources and knowledge, and considering individual needs when designing on-line classes, educators can play a vital role in creating more culturally competent online learning environments. As technological access and knowledge spread among groups of diverse learners, the digital divide will start to lessen. The transfer of knowledge from one member of a community to another is pivotal in helping alleviate the uneven distribution of social capital (Maddison & Lõrincz, 2003, Sein & Furuholt, 2012). Bridging the digital divide and creating multicultural classrooms can be daunting but will eventually lead to more engaged students who learn more in our classrooms (Rawson, 2016).

References

Ahmed, H. S. (2010). Hybrid e-learning acceptance model: Learner perceptions. *Decision Sciences Journal of Innovative Education, 8*(2), 313-346. doi:10.1111/j.1540-4609.2010.00259.

Ayanso, A., Cho, D. I., & Lertwachara, K. (2014). Information and communications technology development and the digital divide: A global and regional assessment. *Information Technology for Development, 20*(1), 60-77. doi:10.1080/02681102.2013.797378.

Benton, T. H. (2009). Online learning: Reaching out to the skeptics. *Chronicle of Higher Education, 56* (4/5), A36-A38.

Booker, K. (2016). Connection and commitment: How sense of belonging and classroom community influence degree persistence for African American undergraduate women. *International Journal of Teaching and Learning in Higher Education, 28*(2), 218-229.

Boysen, G. A. (2012). Teacher and student perceptions of microaggressions in college classrooms. *College Teaching, 60,* 122-129. doi: 10.1080/87567555.2012.654831.

Braverman, B. (2016). The digital divide. *Literacy Today, 33*(4), 16-20.

Cavanaugh, J. K., & Jacquemin, S. J. (2015). A large sample comparison of grade based student learning outcomes in online vs. face-to-face courses. *Online Learning, 19*(2), 25-32.

Chen, B. H., & Chiou, H. (2014). Learning style, sense of community and learning effectiveness in hybrid learning environment. *Interactive Learning Environments, 22*(4), 485-496.

Dewan, S., & Riggins, F. (2005). The digital divide: Current and future research directions. *Journal of the Association for Information Systems, 6*(12), 298-336.

Dole, S., Bloom, L., & Kowalske, K. (2016). Transforming pedagogy: Changing perspectives from teacher-centered to learner-centered. *Interdisciplinary Journal of Problem-Based Learning, 10*(1).

Erickson, F. (2001). Culture in society and in educational practices. In Banks, J.A. & Banks, C.A.M. (Eds.), *Multicultural education: Issues and perspectives* (4th ed.) (pp. 31-58). Hoboken, NJ: John Wiley & Sons.

Kumar, D. (2015). Pros and cons of online education. *NC State White Papers*. Retrieved from https://www.ies.ncsu.edu/resources/white-papers/pros-and-cons-of-online-education/.

Maddison, S., & Lõrincz, G. (2003). Bridging the digital divide. *Computing & Control Engineering, 14*(1), 26.

McComb, S. (2015). Creating risk takers: When teachers support students and create a caring classroom culture, they enable students to take risks. The National Teacher of the Year offers advice on how to make it happen. *Educational Horizons, 93*(3), 9-12 doi:10.1177/0013175X15570853.

Nolan, E. A. (2016). *A critical analysis of multiculturalism, cultural competence, and cultural humility: An examination of potential training opportunities for pre-service teachers* (Doctoral dissertation). Retrieved from Digital Commons at George Fox University. http://digitalcommons.georgefox.edu/cgi/viewcontent.cgi?article=1076&context=edd.

Patel, F. (2014). *Online learning: An educational development perspective*. New York, NY: Nova Science Publishers, Inc.

Rawson, G. (2016). Bridging the digital divide bit by bit. *Capitol Ideas, 59*(3), 38-41.

Salvatore, J., & Shelton, J. N. (2007). Cognitive costs of exposure to racial prejudice. *Psychological Science, 18*(9), 810-815.

Sein, M. K., & Furuholt, B. (2012). Intermediaries: Bridges across the digital divide. *Information Technology for Development, 18*(4), 332-344.

Solórzano, D., Ceja, M., Yosso, T. (2001). Critical race theory, raciamicroaggressions, and campus racial climate: The experiences of African American college students. *Journal of Negro Education, 69*, 60- 73. Retrieved from http://advance.uci.edu/ADVANCE%20PDFs/Climate/CRT_RacialMicros_Campus.pdf.

Stočes, M., Masner, J., & Jarolímek, J. (2015). Mitigation of social exclusion in regions and rural areas: E-learning with focus on content creation and evaluation. *Agris On-Line Papers in Economics & Informatics, 7*(4), 143-150.

Sue, D. W., Lin, A. I., Torino, G. C., Capodilupo, C.M., & Rivera, D. P. (2009). Racial microaggressions and difficult dialogues on race in the classroom. *Cultural Diversity and Ethnic Minority Psychology, 15*, 183-190. doi: 10.1037/a0014191.

Summerville, J. (2005). Developing an online "code of conduct". *AACE Journal, 13*(2), 127-136.

U.S. Department of Education (2016). Degrees and other formal awards conferred surveys. *National Center for Education Statistics, Higher Education General Information Survey (HEGIS)*. Retrieved from https://nces.ed.gov/programs/digest/d16/tables/dt16_322.20.asp?current=yes

U.S. Department of Education (2014). 2003-04, 2007-08, 2011-12 National postsecondary student aid survey. *National Center for Education Statistics.* Retrieved from https://nces.ed.gov/programs/digest/d14/tables/dt14_311.20.asp.

Weimer, M. (2013). *Learner-Centered Teaching: Five Key Changes to Practice*. Jossey-Bass: San Francisco.

Williams, A., Oliver, C., Aumer, K., & Meyers, C. (2016). Racial microaggressions and perceptions of Internet memes. *Computers in Human Behavior, 63*(1), 424-432.

Yurdugül, H., & Menzi Çetin, N. (2015). Investigation of the relationship between learning process and learning outcomes in e-learning environments. *Eurasian Journal of Educational Research, 58*, 57-74.

Chapter Six

Black Men in Higher Education

By Steven Kniffley Truman Harris, Jimmy Joseph,
& DeDe Wohlfarth

Our current educational system poses numerous barriers to Black men at all levels of development. This chapter will use a narrative about a young Black boy named Brandon to demonstrate the challenges to educational success of Black men at the elementary school, middle school, and high school levels. As a result of this institutional racism, Black men are increasingly underrepresented at every level of academic success, and are prone to poor high school graduation rates, as well as college retention and graduation rates.

Dumb. Deviant. Dangerous. These three adjectives are too often used to describe black men in our society. The negative adjectives stereotypically related to Black masculinity are sadly prevalent within an education system where Black males are often considered unintelligent, apathetic, unmotivated, and incapable of learning. Throughout the education of a Black man, he is much more likely than all other genders and ethnicities of children to be perceived as loud, unruly, and a disciplinary problem due to his behavior (Wilson, Hugenberg & Rule, 2017; Dixon, 2008; Duncan, 1976).

A significant manifestation of this negative belief system is the common misperception that there are more Black males in prison than in college. In fact, this statement is patently false (Ryan &

Bauman, 2016; Carson, & Golinelli, 2013). The negative societal perceptions of Black men have been used to simultaneously denigrate their lived experiences as well as justify their non-existence in higher education. Black males can and do make it to college. However, the journey to reaching educational milestones is often filled with pitfalls and traps designed to diminish access to education. Key barriers to Black male education include generationally transmitted learned helplessness in educational settings, false attributions of a racialized masculinity, and ineffective peer leadership. This chapter will explore these barriers using the contextual and developmental narrative of a Black male named Brandon. The narrative follows Brandon from his first day of kindergarten to his first year in college. After reading this chapter, you will be able to identify some of the main barriers and resilience factors associated with the educational journey of Black men.

Developmental Course of Black Men in Education

Elementary School

Brandon is a 5-year-old, dark skinned, Black male with big ears and a wide smile. He is eagerly, and a bit anxiously, entering his first year of school as a kindergartener. Brandon's mom pressed his plaid short-sleeved shirt for his first day of school, and he paired it with an undershirt and baggy shorts—a carefully chosen outfit to reflect his personal sense of fashion and the current style. Brandon will be attending a racially mixed large public elementary school in his city. Brandon is a sociable and friendly active ball of energy who likes dogs and basketball. He lives with his mom and baby sister. His mother works a full-time job as an administrative assistant in the day and a part-time job cleaning offices in the evening. Due to his mother's long work hours, Brandon spends often spends time with his maternal grandmother. His grandmother meets him as he gets off the bus every day and watches him until late in the evening when his mother gets home. His grandmother relies on Brandon to be her helper

and assist with taking care of his baby sister. As Brandon walks with his grandmother and mother to the bus stop the first day of kindergarten, he is unaware of the numerous barriers that may negatively impact his ability to have a successful kindergarten year. These barriers include:
1. The racial discrepancy between students and school staff, administrators, and teachers,
2. The disproportionate use of disciplinary strategies against Black boys, and
3. Widespread culturally unresponsive teaching interventions.

Racial Disparities in the Educational Setting

Brandon attends a racially diverse school, which is increasingly common in our society. The public-school system is undergoing an unprecedented diversification in its student demographics. Over the past 30 years, the number of White students in public schools has decreased by 20% (Mahatmya et al., 2016). At the same time, the percentage of Black and Hispanic students has greatly increased. As of 2010, students of color make up 42% of public school students (Mahatmya et al., 2016). Thus, children are much more likely to attend a racially mixed school, like Brandon does. However, this diversity can be considered both a blessing and a curse. On the downside, children of color are much more likely than White children to have negative educational experiences—including higher teacher turnover, lower school performance, and enrollment in lower-income schools (Loeb, Darling-Hammond & Luczak, 2005; Diamond & Spillane, 2004). However, on the positive side, research shows that mere exposure to cultural diversity increases the likelihood of positive interactions and relationships with culturally diverse individuals (Zebrowitz, White & Wieneke, 2008; Pettigrew & Tropp, 2006). Fortunately for Brandon, the school he attends is mostly Black. Having at least 15% of a student body share the same ethnicity as a student is immeasurably helpful in developing one's racial identity, feeling comfortable at school, and maintaining friends (Syed & Juan, 2012). Brandon attends a neighborhood school that is only a few miles from his home. He already knows some children from his neighborhood—all Black boys—and due to his outgoing and high energy personality, he quickly finds a friendship group within his first few months of school.

The Disproportionate Use of Disciplinary Strategies Against Black Boys

Unfortunately for Brandon, most of his teachers are White females. Compared to Black teachers, White female teachers are much more likely to refer Black boys for special education, discipline Black boys, and overlook them for gifted programs (Ford, 1998). Although Brandon is somewhat likely to have a Black female teacher, he is highly unlikely to have a Black male teacher. Thus, the odds are low that he will have a role model with similar demographic characteristics as himself.

Although Brandon has been met with several disadvantages already, he is smart, a quick learner, and enjoys hands-on learning. He loves recess and sports, especially basketball and football. In his classroom, Brandon often talks out of turn—not due to being disrespectful, but just due to being excited. Brandon has trouble putting on the brakes and scaling down his behavior. By the 2nd month of school, Brandon's mild behavioral problems have already caused him to be sent to the principal's office. Twice. As a kindergartner. Brandon is not alone in being on the receiving end of harsh disciplinary practices. Unfortunately, students of color are likely to experience harsher punishments in response to the same misconduct as their White peers (Aull IV, 2012). This differential treatment in discipline extends to Black boys across the socioeconomic spectrum, with Black male students of all income levels more likely to receive sterner consequences than White male students (Aull IV, 2012). As a powerful national data point to illustrate this problem, consider this: A survey of 72,000 schools found that although Black students made up 18% of the student body in the sampled school, they accounted for a significantly greater percentage of students suspended once (35%) and more than once (46%) (Rudd, 2014). In addition to this, Black students account for approximately 40% of students expelled from school (Rudd, 2014). Rudd's research points to two primary reasons for Black boys receiving harsher punishments: 1) Teacher misperception of student behavior; and 2) A lack of flexibility in disciplinary discretion. For Black male students like Brandon, teachers are more likely to view his behavior as intentionally oppositional, and thus to mete out overly punitive punishments. What causes these misperceptions? Primarily institutional racism with its wide-reaching effects.

Secondly, Rudd (2014) posits that Black boys receive harsher punishments due to a lack of flexibility in disciplinary discretion. Many school systems have adopted "zero tolerance" policies to discipline. A zero tolerance policy is a "non-discretionary approach that mandates a set of often severe, predetermined consequences to student behavior that is applied without regard to the seriousness of behavior, mitigating circumstances, or situational context." (Aull IV, 2012, p. 4). Zero tolerance policies began in the 1990s as a reactionary step to manage serious school behavioral problems, such as weapon or drug possession. Zero policy thinking has spread since its inception, resulting in a paradigm of thinking about discipline that is more punitive than educational. Zero tolerance policy has been strongly indicated in the "school to prison" pipeline (Mallet, 2016). Zero tolerance policies disproportionately negatively affect lower SES students, minority students, and students with disabilities (Mallet, 2016). These policies promote early policy involvement for behavioral problems, as well as labeling children as "troublemakers" from a young age. They serve to make children less engaged in learning and less connected with their schools, essentially alienating them from the educational system at a young age as school becomes associated with personal failure and misconduct. Zero tolerance policies at least partially explain why Black and Latinx students are much more likely to drop out of school as compared to their White peers (Mahatmya et al., 2016). In fact, as early as the third grade, Black students demonstrate significantly lower academic performance than White, Latinx, and Asian children in math and science (West-Olatunji, Behar-Horenstein, Rant, & Cohen-

Philips, 2008). Furthermore, overly harsh punishments contribute to Brandon being perceived negatively by others. Perhaps more ominously, they also contribute to Brandon viewing himself as a "bad kid." The adoption of a felonious identity, which often happens at a young age for Black males, helps to reinforce society's erroneous expectation that Brandon will become a dumb, deviant, and dangerous individual (Swanson, Cunningham & Spencer, 2003). To put this into perspective, Brandon is 5 years old when society begins to narrow its perception of him. He has just lost the first of his baby teeth.

Schools districts can take several steps to reverse the school to prison pipeline, and give children like Brandon a better chance of academic success. For example, schools can implement a tiered intervention points system where different behavioral issues are associated with a certain number of points and subsequent interventions (Zalaznick, 2014). This tiered approach provides teachers and administrators with more flexibility in determining appropriate disciplinary actions. Another successful approach is to collaboratively involve parents, teachers and administrators to create a school's disciplinary procedures. Schools can also implement restorative justice practices that promote peer leadership, self-regulation, and conflict management (Mallet, 2016). Lastly, school districts can develop policies related to community support, conflict resolution, cultural competency, and advanced intervention for at-risk individuals (Mallet, 2016). These factors help increase the educational success of students like Brandon.

Black boys and culturally responsive teaching

To effectively reach and transform the lives of Black male students, teachers must be able to understand and maximize the cultural strengths of each student. However, given the increasingly disproportionate racial makeup of White school teacher's vs Black students, such an understanding is increasingly unlikely (Lopes-Murphy & Murphy, 2016). Many teachers report general discomfort in regards to teaching culturally different students. This is due in part to the overall lack of preparation they receive for managing the challenges of culturally diverse students (Lopes-

Murphy & Murphy, 2016; Mahatmya et al., 2016; West-Olatunji et al., 2008). These challenges highlight the likelihood that a significant number of teachers struggle to engage in culturally responsive teaching practices, even as they learn other research-based pedagogical interventions (Keengwe, 2005). This lack of training in, and district wide lack of support for, culturally responsive teaching practices means that many culturally diverse students will have the deck stacked precariously against them due to the long-reaching effects of our racist society. Research supports that culturally responsive teaching practices can make a substantial difference for children like Brandon and his classmates. The benefits of culturally responsive teaching include: 1.) higher overall levels of effective teaching; 2.) increased connection to student's families, 3.) reduction in student achievement gaps, and 4.) improved fulfilment of accountability requirements (Keengwe, 2005). Additionally, the literature has indicated that culturally responsive teaching can empower students academically, socially, and emotionally (Bustamante, Skidmore, Nelson, & Jones, 2016).

Many models have been developed to address the cultural competency training needs of school teachers (Bustamante et al., 2016; Lindsey, Robins, & Terell, 1999; Schmidt, 1999). These training models share some common components. The best cultural competency teaching interventions share an integration of cultural knowledge content exposure, guided self-reflection, experiential learning, and practical application. Unfortunately, most training programs focus solely on cultural knowledge and do not include the aforementioned other critical components of learning (Bahreman & Swoboda, 2016). In response to this, Brandon's school district considered providing culturally responsive educational training for all of its district's teachers. However, the school district was large and the cost was prohibitive. Instead of providing such training for all of the teachers, they sent two high school teachers—one male and one female, both teachers of color—to the training. Both teachers, Mr. Jones and Ms. Martin, benefited greatly from the training. Unfortunately, Brandon's path would not cross with either of these teachers for many years.

Middle School

As Brandon began middle school, his formidable challenges continued. These challenges will be organized by the following themes: 1. Educational self-fulfilling prophecies; 2. Rise in negative peer influences; and 3. Lack of skill development for goal setting and conflict resolution.

Educational Self-fulfilling Prophecies

Late in his elementary school career, teachers began grouping children by their ability level. Brandon was a bright child, but his academic work never reflected his intelligence. His mom was too busy to push him to do his homework, and his grandmother was too permissive. Brandon would rather go outside or play sports, and unfortunately, his schoolwork tended to reflect his priorities. Brandon was always placed in the "average" student group. Like most kids who are not in the high achieving group, the nature of Brandon's lessons changed. Classes became more about rote memorization with less critical thinking about interesting problems (Valli, Croninger & Buese, 2012). As a result of this ability grouping, Brandon's teachers did not expect very much of him in terms of his school work. These lower expectations occur because teachers also are more likely to be critical and have more conflicts with children who are not in the highest achieving groups. This lack of high expectations further reduced Brandon's achievement level. He fell victim to an educational self-fulfilling prophecy (McKown, Gregory & Weinstein, 2010). In other words, after incorporating his teachers' negative views about him, Brandon became less and less motivated to do well at school, and began to believe that he was unintelligent. By 3rd grade, Brandon came to believe he was truly dumb. By 5th grade, Brandon's teachers recommended that he be placed in the lowest ability level group. He wasn't motivated to do well in school and his B's and C's had slipped to mostly D's and U's. Brandon's mother was frustrated with his grades, and threatened to smack him if he didn't change his ways. However, his mother was too exhausted after work to follow up with monitoring his school grades, let alone to summon the strength to whip him. Honestly, she was exhausted. Parent teacher conferences and other chances for her to get involved in Brandon's education came and went. Like many other parents with hourly wage jobs, Brandon's mom could not easily take off work without getting docked in pay for missing an hour of productivity. Indeed, research suggests that lower SES parents are less likely to be involved with their children's academic endeavors (Diamond, 1999; Jeynes, 2007).

Rise in Negative Peer Influences

Brandon didn't just come to believe he was dumb. He also began to see himself as a juvenile delinquent. Like most of us, Brandon became friends with the people whom he saw the most. Familiarity, similarity, and geographic convenience are the most common reasons we become friends with others. Brandon didn't intend to start hanging out with the "bad" kids, but his peer group became Black boys who acted up in class. The children who were in the low level academic group, and who lived in his neighborhood just happened to be the ones he saw the most.

Brandon also played sports throughout elementary and middle school. He would happily go from football to basketball to track seasons throughout the academic year. Brandon was motivated to play sports, but as he grew older, the expectations for sports intensified in terms of the number of practices, the expectations of travel teams, and the general cost of the process. In 5th grade, his basketball uniform cost $225. His mom just didn't have the money for him to keep playing sports, and his grandmother didn't have the time to shuttle him back and forth from practices. By the end of middle school, Brandon was no longer participating in any organized school sports, but he still loved to play basketball with his friends.

Lack of Skill Development for Goal Setting and Conflict Resolution

As Brandon quit playing sports, he grew less connected with school than ever. In 7th grade, Brandon's grandmother died unexpectedly of a heart attack. Brandon was devastated. His grandmother had been his caregiver for years—she was like a second mom to him. Brandon decided he wasn't saddened by his grandmother's death, but was instead angry. The masculine expectations that came with being a Black male offered no room for Brandon to express sadness or grief. Society only allowed him to feel anger, and so he expressed it through fighting and aggression.

Brandon became a well-respected bully—a socially prominent, well-liked child despite his bullying (Vailancourt et al., 2010b). To ensure that he kept his high social status, Brandon deliberately targeted children he perceived of as weak, and thus those who his classmates were least likely to defend (Veenstra et al., 2010). As Brandon continued to engage in bullying, his opportunities to engage in social problem solving and positive conflict resolution were lost. Brandon began to perceive even unintentional slights by other children as hostile acts, and felt that his social status and budding masculinity would be negatively affected if he didn't respond with aggression to such perceived hostile acts (Meece & Mize, 2011). Brandon goals also changed. Like many young men of color, Brandon realized that the odds of educational, career, or financial success were significantly stacked against him (OECD, 2013a). Over time, his belief in his ability to succeed in a system that he rightly perceived as rigged against him eroded. Instead of investing in his education or a career, Brandon began looking for ways to make a quick dollar, an understandable decision with steep consequences, as he began to spend time with others already involved in criminal activities.

High School

After wearily navigating all of these challenges, a jaded, cynical, and exhausted young boy began high school. Still well-dressed in tight athletic shirts, sagging jeans and expensive shoes, Brandon began his first day of high school with a long bus ride. Brandon's years in high school represent a pivotal four years in his development and will ultimately impact the trajectory for the rest of his life in regards to employment, financial security, physical and mental health, and future academic endeavors. However, in many ways, the odds are stacked against Brandon. Brandon's challenges in high school are summarized under one broad theme, demonstrated by the primary task of adolescence of finding one's identity (Berk & Meyers, 2015).

Renegotiation of Identity from Scholar to Thug

Black males are at the bottom of four-year high school graduation rates in 35 states. During the 2012-2013 academic year, the graduation rate for Black males was a dismal 59% (OECD, 2013a). Since that time, the graduation gap between Black males and White males has increased significantly (Ryan & Bauman, 2016). In high school, Brandon will confront a racialized masculinity identity crisis, coupled with limited feelings of school belonging and a perceived narrowing of life choices post-high school.

As Brandon navigates high school, he will dramatically renegotiate his racialized masculinity as he explores what it means to be a Black man. Throughout his life, Brandon has received competing messages about what it means to be Black from his peers, family, and popular culture. Some messages were positive, including messages of cultural pride to help navigate his daily experiences of racism and discrimination. However, many of the messages Brandon has received are limiting and place Brandon in a cultural box, including the perception that he, as a Black male, is dumb, deviant, and dangerous. Brandon tries to manage his identity conflict by seeking approval and validation from his peers for his hyper-masculine behavior, relying on popular culture to inform his vision of what a Black male is supposed to be. One critical component of society's definition of Black masculinity is disengagement with education. In fact, this disengagement includes an almost complete severance of school belongingness

(McKown, Gregory, & Weinstein, 2010). School belonging describes a student's degree of positive affiliation with his or her school. School belongingness is associated with high levels of academic engagement and achievement, motivation, psychological well-being, and low levels of problem behaviors (McKown, Gregory, & Weinstein, 2010).

Brandon has spent his academic career in a covertly hostile environment. Without directly saying it, the school environment has communicated that Brandon's cultural background is viewed as a negative—a risk factor, a problem. Educational negativity toward Black males contributes to their reduced academic expectations, as well as increasingly punitive punishments for misbehavior. Brandon is thus less motivated to achieve academically and is less likely to comply with school rules. Brandon has internalized the message that others don't care about him, so he has no reason to care about them. Brandon has only one exception to this mutually negative situation. Remember back in elementary school when the school district sent two teachers of color to receive training in culturally responsive teaching? In 11th grade US history, Brandon finally meets one of these teachers: A Black man named Mr. Jones who teaches American history in a way that challenges students to think of historical perspectives rarely considered by the traditional teaching of history, including through the eyes of women, Black slaves, and Native people. Mr. Jones also teaches critical pedagogy, or the idea that people need to confront current societal "isms" to create social change instead of just accepting the status quo.

Brandon is mesmerized by Mr. Jones. He is the first Black role model that Brandon has ever had in his entire educational career. Brandon is engaged in class discussions and actually works hard in his class. One day after class, Mr. Jones asks to speak to Brandon one-on-one. For the first time in his life, Brandon hears the words "college potential," although he is not sure what to do with this information. Mr. Jones has provided Brandon with a singular and lonely voice to combat a chorus of voices that continue to echo negative expectations for Brandon. Unfortunately,

Mr. Jones's singular voice is not loud enough to rise over the din, and Brandon feels that his choices post-high school are severely limited. Long gone are the days where Brandon aspired to be a doctor, lawyer, or some other type of professional. Instead, life circumstances, popular culture, and peer influences, have narrowly focused Brandon's career aspirations on immediate survival and "quick money." Brandon's post-high school choices have additionally been impacted by his lack of Black male role models. For example, as a younger child, Brandon really liked dogs and thought about becoming a veterinarian. However, Brandon never met a Black veterinarian, so he decided such a career was unrealistic. Instead, Brandon has been inundated with images of Black men as entertainers or athletes, neither of which require educational success. Brandon's graduation from high school should have been a celebration. After all, he had defied so many odds just to get to this milestone. Unfortunately, he staggered across the finish line with a 1.2. GPA, which was brought up to that level only by his "A" performance in Mr. Jones's class. The night of graduation, however, Brandon went out with some friends to celebrate and the celebration got out of hand. Brandon was arrested for DUI, but, as a 17-year-old, his first arrest was not recorded on his permanent record, despite the negative effect it had on his insurance premiums.

First Year of College

Brandon didn't go to college right after high school. In fact, his attending college at all was something of a fluke. Brandon had been arrested once after age 18, in the summer right after he graduated high school. He was carrying a weapon without a permit as he had regularly began doing since he felt unsafe without his gun. Brandon was having trouble making money, so he took a job at a chain coffee shop that strove to hire diverse people with criminal records. The coffee shop was willing to hire him based on a strong recommendation from Mr. Jones. After six months working at the coffee shop, company policy paid for employees to attend college. Brandon decided to take a class at the local community college, mostly because it was free and because the hot barista with whom he worked told him that she was attending classes at the community college and working towards an Associate's Degree. Brandon decided that he had a better chance of having a relationship with his co-worker if she saw him as an intelligent college man. Brandon had always felt like a salmon swimming upstream in school, and his first week at the community college was no exception. Including his co-worker, Brandon was one of three Black people in his class, and the only Black male. He walked into the Contemporary Literature class and felt the eyes of every student fixed on him. Their eyes looked right through him, as if to say, "You don't belong here." Brandon already felt this way, of course, because of years and years of failing in school. He thought back to first day of kindergarten, when he so carefully selected his outfit: Was he ever really happy in school? Did he ever belong in school? Brandon's class was assigned *The Color Purple* by Alice Walker. Brandon listened to his classmates as they discussed the book, and thought to himself, "They just don't get it." He meant that White people had no clue what it meant to be Black. Like many other Black students, Brandon found that many White students, and sadly, professors, tended to vilify, criticize and belittle his culture (Smith, Mustaffa, Jones, Curry & Allen, 2016; Sue, Capodilupo & Holder, 2008), although often in covert and dismissive ways. Instead of acquiescing in his Literature class, however, Brandon recalled the powerful voice of Mr. Jones and challenged the racism in the classroom. However, his classmates quickly shut him down, accused him of being "oversensitive" and "playing the race card" (Sue, 2016). Brandon quickly reverted to his adolescent self, and decided that he must quickly protect his masculine image by instead denying the pain he was experiencing in response to his classmates' invalidating comments. He convinced himself that he didn't care about his classmates and stopped speaking.

Gaslighting, the collective response of individuals unwilling to acknowledge the lived experience of an entire culture, has shut him down (Bush, 2004; Nadal, Wong, Griffin, Davidoff & Sriken,

2014). Furthermore, such daily experiences with racism erode self-esteem, particularly in Black males (Nadal, Wong, Griffin, Davidoff & Sriken, 2014). Brandon is attempting to keep hold of the culture that defines very important aspects of himself, while at the same time integrating the values and maxims of another culture that continually berates and vilifies his own culture—an excruciatingly difficult process. It becomes easier for him to quit than try. Shortly thereafter, he stops attending class, telling his attractive co-worker that school just isn't for him. In fact, if Brandon stayed in school, it may have been at his own expense. When an individual must work to challenge gender or racial norms, especially in the context of a skeptical audience, his or her self-regulatory abilities began to wane (Vohs, Baumeister & Ciarocco, 2005). The resulting negative effects of maintaining such a self-presentation include reduced concentration and psychological well-being, including decreased overall self-esteem. Thus, the cycle has come full circle: Brandon has internalized society's messages about Black men, and is now at high risk for stereotype threat as well as the imposter syndrome (Cokley, McClain, Enciso & Martinez, 2013; Steele & Aronson, 1995). Brandon was never afforded the same benefits and privileges as those in the majority culture. His failure thus does not reflect his lack of ability, or a lack of motivation. Instead, Brandon has come to believe that Black men do not belong in higher education. He has failed in a system which was never constructed for him to succeed, adding to the already alarming statistics of Black men who fail in our educational system, or perhaps more accurately, are failed by our educational system.

References

Aull IV, E. H. (2012). Zero tolerance, frivolous juvenile court referrals, and the school-to-prison pipeline: Using arbitration as a screening-out method to help plug the pipeline. *Ohio St. J. on Disp. Resol., 27*, 179.

Bahreman, N. T., & Swoboda, S. M. (2016). Honoring Diversity: Developing Culturally Competent Communication Skills Through Simulation. *The Journal of Nursing Education, 55*(2), 105-108. doi:10.3928/01484834-20160114-09

Berk, L., & Meyers, A. (2015). *Infants, children and adolescents.* Boston: Pearson.

Bush, M. E. (2004). Race, ethnicity, and Whiteness. In *Sage Race Relations Abstracts* (Vol. 29, No. 3-4, pp. 5-48).

Bustamante, R. M., Skidmore, S. T., Nelson, J. A., & Jones, B. E. (2016). Evaluation of a Cultural Competence Assessment for Preservice Teachers. *The Teacher Educator, 51*(4), 297-313.

Carson, E. A., & Golinelli, D. (2013). Prisoners in 2012: Trends in admissions and releases, 1991–2012. *Washington DC: Bureau of Justice Statistics.*

Cokley, K., McClain, S., Enciso, A., & Martinez, M. (2013). An examination of the impact of minority status stress and impostor feelings on the mental health of diverse ethnic minority college students. *Journal of Multicultural Counseling and Development, 41*(2), 82-95

Diamond, J. B. (1999). Beyond social class: Cultural resources and educational participation among low-income Black parents. *Berkeley Journal of Sociology,* 15-54.

Diamond, J. B., & Spillane, J. P. (2004). High-stakes accountability in urban elementary schools: Challenging or reproducing inequality? *Teachers College Record, 106*(6), 1145-1176.

Dixon, T. L. (2008). Crime news and racialized beliefs: Understanding the relationship between local news viewing and perceptions of African Americans and crime. *Journal of Communication, 58*(1), 106-125.

Duncan, B. L. (1976). Differential social perception and attribution of intergroup violence: Testing the lower limits of stereotyping of Blacks. *Journal of Personality & Social Psychology, 34*(4), 590.

Ford, D. Y. (1998). The underrepresentation of minority students in gifted education problems and promises in recruitment and retention. *The Journal of Special Education, 32*(1), 4-14.

Jeynes, W. H. (2007). The relationship between parental involvement and urban secondary school student academic achievement: A meta-analysis. *Urban education, 42*(1), 82-110.

Keengwe, J. (2005, June). E-learning: The Benefits, the Challenges and the Future. In *EdMedia: World Conference on Educational Media and Technology* (Vol. 2005, No. 1, pp. 3935-3939).

Lindsay, R. B., Robins, K. N., & Terrell, R. D. (1999). Cultural literacy: A manual for school leaders. *Corwin, Thousand Oaks.*

Loeb, S., Darling-Hammond, L., & Luczak, J. (2005). How teaching conditions predict teacher turnover in California schools. *Peabody Journal of Education, 80*(3), 44-70.

Lopes-Murphy, S. A., & Murphy, C. G. (2016). The Influence of Cross-Cultural Experiences & Location on Teachers' Perceptions of Cultural Competence. *Journal of the Scholarship of Teaching and Learning, 16*(3), 57-71.

Mahatmya, D., Lohman, B., Brown, E., & Conway-Turner, J. (2016). The role of race and teachers' cultural awareness in predicting low-income, Black and Hispanic students' perceptions of educational attainment. *Social Psychology of Education, 19*(2), 427. doi:10.1007/s11218-016-9334-1

Mallett, C. A. (2016). The school-to-prison pipeline: From school punishment to rehabilitative inclusion. *Preventing School Failure: Alternative Education for Children and Youth, 60*(4), 296-304.

McKown, C., Gregory, A., & Weinstein, R. S. (2010). Expectations, stereotypes, and self-fulfilling prophecies in classroom and school life. *Handbook of research on schools, schooling, and human development,* 256-274.

Meece, D., & Mize, J. (2011). Preschoolers' cognitive representations of peer relationships: Family origins and behavioural correlates. *Early Childhood Development and Care, 181,*63-72.

Nadal, K. L., Wong, Y., Griffin, K. E., Davidoff, K., & Sriken, J. (2014). The adverse impact of racial microaggressions on college students' self-esteem. *Journal of college student development, 55*(5), 461-474.

OECD (Organization for Economic Cooperation and Development). (2013a). Education at a glance 2013: OECD Indicators. Retrieved from www.oecd.org/edu/eag2013.

Pettigrew, T. F., & Tropp, L. R. (2006). A meta-analytic test of intergroup contact theory. *Journal of Personality & Social Psychology, 90*(5), 751.

Rudd, T. (2014). Racial disproportionality in school discipline: Implicit bias is heavily implicated. *Kirwan Institute for the Study of Race and Ethnicity. Retrieved from: http://kirwaninstitute.osu.edu/wp-content/uploads/2014/02/racial-disproportionalityschools-02.pdf.*

Ryan, C. L., & Bauman, K. (2016). Educational attainment in the United States: 2015. *Current Population Reports,* 20.

Schmidt, P. L. (1999). *Understanding American and German business cultures: a manager's guide to the cultural context in which American and German companies operate.* Meridian World Press.

Smith, W. A., Mustaffa, J. B., Jones, C. M., Curry, T. J., & Allen, W. R. (2016). 'You make me wanna holler and throw up both my hands!': Campus culture, Black misandric microaggressions, and racial battle fatigue. *International Journal of Qualitative Studies in Education, 29*(9), 1189-1209.

Steele, C. M., & Aronson, J. (1995). Stereotype threat and the intellectual test performance of African Americans. *Journal of Personality & Social Psychology, 69*(5), 797.

Sue, D. W. (2016). *Race talk and the conspiracy of silence: Understanding and facilitating difficult dialogues on race.* John Wiley & Sons.

Sue, D. W., Capodilupo, C. M., & Holder, A. (2008). Racial microaggressions in the life experience of Black Americans. *Professional Psychology: Research and Practice, 39*(3), 329.

Swanson, D. P., Cunningham, M., & Spencer, M. B. (2003). Black males' structural conditions, achievement patterns, normative needs, and "opportunities". *Urban Education, 38*(5), 608-633.

Syed, M., & Juan, M.J. (2012). Birds of an ethnic feather? Ethnic identity homophily among college-age friends. *Journal of Adolescence, 35,* 1505-1514.

Vailancourt, T., McDougall, P., Hymel, S., & Sunderani, S. (2010b). Respect or fear? The relationship between power and bullying behavior. In S.R. Jimerson, S.M.

Swearer, & D. L. Espelage (Eds.) Handbook of bullying in schools: An international perspective (pp. 211-222). NewYork: Routledge.

Valli, L., Croninger, R. G., & Buese, D. (2012). Studying High-Quality Teaching in a Highly Charged Policy Environment. *Teachers College Record, 114*(4), n4.

Veenstra, R., Lindenburg, S., Munniksma, A., & Dijkstra, J.K. (2010). The complex relation between bullying, victimization, acceptance, and rejection: Given special attention to status, affection, and sex differences. *Child Development, 81,* 480-486.

Vohs, K. D., Baumeister, R. F., & Ciarocco, N. J. (2005). Self-regulation and self-presentation: regulatory resource depletion impairs impression management and effortful self-presentation depletes regulatory resources. *Journal of Personality & Social Psychology, 88*(4), 632.

West-Olatunji, C. A., Behar-Horenstein, L., Rant, J., & Cohen-Phillips, L. N. (2008). Enhancing cultural competence among teachers of African American children using mediated lesson study. *The Journal of Negro Education,* 27-38.

Wilson, J. P., Hugenberg, K., & Rule, N. O. (2017). Racial Bias in Judgments of Physical Size and Formidability: From Size to Threat. *Journal of Personality & Social Psychology.* Advance online publication.

Zalaznick, M. (2014). Closing the school-to-prison PIPELINE. *District Administration, 50*(10), 34.

Zebrowitz, L. A., White, B., & Wieneke, K. (2008). Mere exposure and racial prejudice: Exposure to other-race faces increases liking for strangers of that race. *Social Cognition, 26*(3), 259-275.

Chapter 7

Allowing for a Silent Pause: Introverts in Higher Education

By Meena Kumar, Nisha Kumar, & DeDe Wohlfarth

Many diverse cultures value reflection and a silent pause before speaking. However, typical North American classroom environments place a high value on extroversion. Therefore, classrooms are primarily comprised of activities that facilitate students' extroverted qualities, such as class participation points, large group discussion, and classroom presentations. Introverted students are perceived as less interested in learning than extroverts, as they are unable to effectively use their strengths in the classroom. Further, research supports cognitive and biological differences between introverts and extroverts that impact their learning in college classrooms. This chapter discusses research regarding introversion in the classroom and suggests practical suggestions for professors to better meet the learning needs of introverted students.

Your authors for this chapter (Kumar & Kumar) are twin sisters, both pursuing doctoral degrees on opposite sides of the country. We are both Indian-American, born and raised in the United States. Our family and culture prizes education above all else. Since childhood, we realized that we must meet high academic standards to please our family, including ensuring that we achieve all A grades, despite the considerable effort to achieve this goal. In addition, we were always expected to meet familial and societal standards in regards to our dress, poise, and composure. We have learned to listen and respect our elders without adding our own opinions to family discussions. Whenever one of us spoke too quickly or too often, we learned through feedback from our family that a far better way to respond was by remaining quiet, listening, and adhering to Indian-American cultural expectations regarding our behavior and personality. Both of us learned that if we said something, it must be both "right" and add value to the conversation. We thus learned to pause carefully before any comment, taking the time to self-reflect and self-assess.

While we could take solace that our parents could understand and appreciate our quiet nature, as they too are introverted, we have both received the message early on in life from others outside of our immediate family that our quiet personalities were a negative trait. This has never been more apparent than in the classroom. In our North American classrooms, our teachers demand that we speak our minds and discuss topics with our classmates, oftentimes focusing on topics without clear resolutions or "right" answers. We are expected to spontaneously pose questions and even challenge the professor. We are supposed to talk instead of just taking notes. Since elementary school, we have duly received the message that the very qualities so valued in our family and culture were actually hindering our academic success.

Every time both of us entered a classroom, we became self-conscious, anticipating that we would be unable to meet the societal expectations of a student in the United States. These expectations typically include contributing verbally to the discussion, asking questions, and providing opinions or ideas. We often have laughed at our similar shared experiences from 2000 miles apart: During class discussions, I initially happily absorb the material and listen to the contributions of others. As the class progresses, I become increasingly anxious, hyperaware of who has spoken and who has not. Often, I am the sole holdout, or at best, one of the few only students, who have yet to speak in class. I sit uncomfortably in my seat, anticipating the dreadful moment when the professor will eventually ask anyone who has not verbally shared to do so. If this does not occur, I breathe a sigh of relief. However, my own internalized expectations based on the extroverted ideal remind me that I have failed once again. I leave the class with a sinking feeling in my stomach, as if the world's fate depended on my class participation and I, once again, had failed the world miserably.

We were both always good students based on the high quality of our written work. However, any positive evaluations we received were always immediately followed by a comment about our lack of verbal participation. If so many teachers across so many years agreed that our reticence to speak was a problem that needed to be solved, then we definitely needed to fix the problem.

Being excellent students who wanted to succeed, we tried to improve the situation. We spent hours reading and rereading book chapters, reflecting on the material before class, and preparing comments and questions in advance. We tried to comment in class, because we knew how important it was. The pauses never seemed long enough. However, while our participation improved somewhat, it was never comparable to many other students. On the rare times that one of us did speak, we were so focused on speaking that we would forget to listen to other students or reflect on the material, which was, of course, a detriment to learning. Over time, we both felt hopeless and defeated by our failed efforts. School was no longer about a love for learning but about conforming to a particular standard that seemed unreachable, despite our best efforts. Although we shared a passion to obtain knowledge, study hard, and advance in our education, we oftentimes wondered whether the introvert qualities we possessed were incompatible with the vision of our futures.

How would we ever succeed in reaching our educational goals if classrooms valued extroversion over introversion? This question forms the heart of this chapter: Addressing how cultural differences in the valuing of extroversion and introversion can affect students' learning in the classroom. Indeed, we know that extroverted classrooms made learning more difficult for us, and we hope to encourage professors to recreate their classrooms to encourage more silent pauses.

Imagine a student who consistently raises their hand and

contributes to class discussion. Is this student interested and engaged in the class? Most teachers would say yes. Now, imagine a student who is quiet, does not make eye contact with the teacher, and is fiddling with her phone, simultaneously texting a friend while checking her Facebook status. Is this student engaged in the material? I'm sure many would agree that this student is unmotivated or disengaged from the class. However, how about the student who is also quiet but consistently makes eye contact with others, takes notes, and nods frequently? Is this student learning? Is she interested in the material?

When a child enters schooling in the Western world, values of extroversion become the norm. Values of extroversion relevant to the classroom context include learning through talking, thinking aloud, being assertive, as well as presenting one's self as sociable (Cain & Klein, 2015). If a student speaks up and shares commentary, this student is demonstrating that she read the material, is engaged in the class, and is actively participating in her own learning. Teachers then perceive this student's high levels of class participation as evidence that she is learning and thinking. So, teachers grade class participation, use class discussion, and assign class presentations as benchmarks to determine if students are learning. However, introverts who are reserved, self-reflective, and become drained by social stimulation, are less inclined to participate verbally and are penalized for their silence. They are viewed as less engaged, withdrawn, and less interested in learning. Verbal participation is not only reinforced, but viewed as essential classroom behavior.

Whether in social groups or classrooms, introverts may want to learn but do not feel that the classroom environment is conducive to their strengths. Thus, introverts may not want to further their education, believing that academics is not for them because of its high social demands. However, setting academic goals should be based on one's own specific interests rather than perceptions that academia is only for the extroverts. Introverts can have an important place in academia if they choose, but the current structure of classrooms does not reward qualities typically associated with introversion. As introverts with common personal experiences, we can attest that rising to third year doctoral level education has not been easy for us because of typical current classroom structures.

Note that, in this chapter, we will be using the terms "extrovert" and "introvert" in order to identify those who gain energy by being around other people and those who gain energy by being alone, respectively. Both personality types highly value social connection. However, introverts are better able to engage in and contribute to social relationships by spending time alone or engaging in quiet activities, either before or after the social experience, or ideally, both before and after. Introverts find being around others constantly a draining experience; extroverts find being alone boring or lonely. Our chapter is geared to the quiet voices who are just as crucial to society as the loud ones and who deserve to be valued and heard. The concept of introversion is crucial to developing cultural competence because of the numerous cultures represented by students of diversity that value introversion over extroversion, silence over conversation, reflection over exuberance, and restraint over jack-rabbit responding. In other words, many cultures represented by students of color value the benefits of silent pause.

Objectives of Chapter

The purpose of this chapter is to understand personality differences within students and use this knowledge to tailor classroom instruction to meet the needs of introverted students.

Brief Literature Review

If we conjure an image of a typical classroom, we typically imagine students raising their hand and teachers calling on them to answer questions. In fact, this image is easily found on the internet when searching for pictures of teaching and learning. Despite this prototypical image, many other typical behaviors of the classroom environment are not immediately apparent. For example, classrooms tend to include many environmental stimuli, such as PowerPoint visual images, the roar of the air conditioning unit, and side conversations. Thus, this classroom environment may be distracting to an introvert while being ignored as mere background noise to an extrovert. Research supports that introverts generally prefer less distracting environments (Furnham, Gunter, & Peterson, 1994).

However, a critical question to ask is whether introverts learn better in low stimulation environments. Silence is most conducive to optimal performance on complex cognitive tasks. In fact, even the presence of music or background noises can detract from performance on difficult tasks. However, introverts' performance is markedly negatively affected by background noise compared to extroverts, whose performance on complex cognitive tasks, such as arithmetic and reading comprehension, was largely unaffected by background noise, even when controlling for cognitive ability (Dobbs, Furnham, & McClelland, 2011; Furnham, Gunter, & Peterson, 1994). Extroverts also were quicker to react on a cognitive task when arousal was high, while introverts were quicker to react when arousal was low (Matthews, 2009). In other words, a high-energy atmosphere, such as a classroom with a Jeopardy style quiz game, motivates extroverts to perform well while simultaneously overwhelming introverts, who perform particularly poorly. These results support the key ideas that introverts struggle to perform at their best under highly stimulating environments, while extroverts perform well, maybe even thrive, in environments that provide high stimulation (Schmeck & Lockhart, 1983). Consider the implication of this research on high-energy and active learning classrooms, and it will hopefully cause a silent pause as you re-examine your own classroom.

Rewards and punishments are highly structured within the academic world – they are used to ensure that students are making efforts to succeed in a course. A typical syllabus offers extra points for participation and reduced points for failure for contribute to class discussions. Thus, if a student speaks up in class, she is tangibly rewarded with participation points, and if she fails to do so, she is punished by not receiving participation points. However, different factors motivate extroverts and introverts. Indeed, powerful neuroscientific research of personality traits indicates differences in brain activity between introverts and extroverts (Mueller et al., 2014; Smillie, Cooper, & Pickering, 2011). An extrovert typically responds well to external positive rewards, such as money, with increasingly more dopamine, the "reward chemical," than is true for introverts. Introverts are less motivated by such external rewards.

Let's go back to the class participation example. If an extroverted student makes one comment in class, she will likely receive positive praise from other students and her teacher as well as class participation points. This positive reward for participation energizes the extroverted student by providing a burst of dopamine. The extrovert will then continue to make comments and contribute verbally even more with every reward. In fact, she may begin making superficial, nonsensical, or tangential comments only because of the powerful social and tangible reinforcers she is receiving, becoming essentially addicted to the high of making such comments, instead of her comments actually being correlated with meaningful learning.

An introvert may make one comment in a class. However, this one comment is draining for her, as she does not experience that dopamine increase from rewards as significantly as extroverts do. Highly extroverted people, upon receiving a random reward, gave more positive feedback via brain activity than introverts (Smillie, Cooper, & Pickering, 2011). An introvert not only reacts differently to rewards than extroverts, but also to punishments. Introverts are more sensitive to negative feedback than extroverts when a reward is possible (Mueller et al., 2014). Thus, extroverts are less sensitive to failure during performance-based tasks as measured by their brain activity. In the classroom, introverts understandably, then, are more hesitant to speak in class, as perceived failure is more damaging to them than their extroverted classmates. Thus, typical American classrooms are stacked against introverts' success, and learning, in multiple ways.

According to a literature review summarizing the relevant

research (Matthews, 2009), extroverts are also able to successfully divide their attention between tasks, recall information from short-term memory more quickly, resist distraction, and are quicker in movement and more fluent in speech production than introverts. Introverts are more vigilant, better at recalling information from long-term memory, and are quicker and more accurate in problem-solving tasks than extroverts. Since introverts appear to learn or react differently to certain classroom contexts, those classrooms that favor extroverts, which often describes many college classrooms, make learning more difficult for introverts.

Educational systems and teachers largely have accepted that verbal class participation results in increased learning. The limited research conducted on this topic indicates that class participation is associated with understanding course content (Carstens et al., 2016; Murray & Lang, 1997). On the surface, then, this research seems to supports the association between verbal participation and learning. However, are the students who participate more frequently actually learning more than those who participated less? An alternative hypothesis is that low participators are not only engaging in non-speaking behavior, but are also not actively engaged in the classroom in alternative ways, such as listening to others and the teacher, and taking notes. If these non-attentive students could be separated from quiet-but-engaged students, the research conclusions may be different.

An additional problem to this research is that test scores are not the best barometer of student learning. The research, however, does clearly support that extroverted students are more successful in achieving grades (i.e., rewards) than introverted students. In other words, classroom environments and expectations typically mesh well with extroverts and fosters their achievement. Yet, the research results do not support that extroverts are somehow better learners than others or that they retained the material once they learned it.

Another problem with the typical extroverted American classroom is that it does not consider values of collectivistic cultures that may conflict with Western values of class participation. According to Markus and Kitayama (1991), individualistic cultures prioritize the self over others in the social context. Thus, the needs of the self generally outweigh the needs of others in society. Alternatively, collectivistic cultures prioritize the group over the individual. Thus, the needs of the group or family tend to outweigh the needs of the individual. Asian cultures, as well as cultures of Argentina and Brazil, traditionally value collectivistic thinking. North American and European cultures fall squarely on the individualistic dimension.

Thus, in a classroom context, individualistic cultures such as the United States nurture and reward the open sharing of individual perspectives and opinions. By contrast, collectivistic cultures value harmony and respect within the classroom. Because of Confucian values of respect for elders, Chinese learners view their teachers as the receptacle of knowledge from whom they must learn. In addition, Chinese culture values ensuring that others' social status is preserved, so that every effort is made to ensure that teachers do not "lose face" (Kennedy, 2002). In Chinese classrooms, class participation in which students openly discuss their opinions is seen as selfish; challenging others, and the teacher, is viewed as disrespectful. In a traditional North American cultural classroom, personal stories and individual opinions are shared freely, debates are common, and challenging authority by asking questions is expected. Of course, some North American cultures, such as Native American cultures, also value respect and collectivism (Pewewardy, 2002), but the traditional Northern American classroom typically favors individualism over collectivism. Overall, one's cultural background shapes expectations and norms regarding classroom behavior, which has implications for student learning.

Introverts' biological, cognitive, and cultural differences directly relate to their classroom behavior. In small group work, introverts contributed more comments that were collaborative in nature, while extroverts made more comments that were argumentative in nature (Nussbaum, 2002). Introverts from collectivistic cultures may feel particularly uncomfortable sharing ideas and opinions that may conflict with others. Nussbaum's study was one of the few to highlight differences in the quality or content of introverts' participation rather than just the frequency of participation. Introverts, then, are contributing to discussion, just in a very different way than extroverts, and one that is not easily rewarded by tally marks for higher levels of participation.

Previous research robustly supports active learning, an instructional method that allows students to think meaningfully about class material within the classroom (Prince, 2004). On the surface, introvert qualities and values seem to conflict with active learning paradigms that require student engagement and participation. Many teachers would believe that introverts prefer passive teacher-led instruction. Active learning is usually contrasted with passive learning, where students are receiving information in teacher-led instruction. However, active learning is not just more activities, higher levels of engagement, or even more participation by students. Rather, active learning involves having students engage in specific activities that align with the teacher's objectives and encourage students to think critically and deeply, regardless of the students' level of movement within the classroom (Weimer, 2013). Then, active learning need not be synonymous with verbal class participation. This is good news for introverts. Introverts enjoy reflective thinking, and a classroom that emphasizes active learning also focuses on reflective thinking.

Active learning is important in the classroom for all students, regardless of personality type (Weimer, 2013). However, introverts may be more uncomfortable in some environments that promote active learning, as many of the activities are geared towards extroverts. Active learning does not inherently demand constant verbal participation or class discussion. Instead, students can be engaged in active learning while completing challenging thought-provoking worksheets or writing one minute papers (Weimer, 2013). The key is for professors to choose at least some active learning classroom activities that play to the self-reflective strengths and low stimulation needs of introverts. As is true for most of life, a balance is good.

Practical Solutions: Silent Pauses

What does active learning for introverts look like? The following are modified versions of pedagogical tools that emphasize active learning and are well-suited for introverts' many strengths:

Cafeteria plan for assignments. Students choose to take college classes for different reasons. Some students may sign up for a class to check off one of their language arts credits or to further their knowledge in science as a precursor to medical school. Others may be genuinely interested in the subject matter. Thus, students' goals and objectives differ. Providing students with high levels of choice in assignments allows them to take charge of their own learning – and to identify what they want to achieve in terms of this learning. How is this related to the conversation about introverts? Many introverts, although they desire to learn, are highly sensitive to the possibility of failing to meet the teacher's expectations listed in the syllabus (e.g., class participation, presentations, etc.). This sensitivity to negative feedback results in introverts feeling uncomfortable in classes and avoiding taking learning risks, which hampers their learning (Mueller et al., 2014). Introverts also tend to prefer work that is meaningful to them, even if this work is difficult or time-consuming (Lambert, 2003). Thus, creating their own class goals and engaging in the assignments that align with their strengths provides numerous benefits to introverts, including: 1. Feeling more comfortable in the class as they are able to meet realistic goals, instead of feeling pressured to meet unrealistic goals; 2. Feeling validated that they are not required to speak publicly; and 3. Gently encouraging introverts to step outside of their comfort zone if willing to do so. Once an introvert selects a goal and realizes that an assignment that requires some public speaking or collaboration would benefit her learning, she will be more likely to perform well on these assignments. However, the key is providing some degree of choice to students who can then decide which assignments will best enable them to learn.

Self-reflective in-class assignments. Class is usually reserved for teacher-led lecture and large-group discussion. However, these in-class instructional methods are as draining for introverts as they are highly stimulating for extroverts. Introverts require more time than their extroverted counterparts to process information in class (Dobbs, Furnham, & McClelland, 2011; Furnham, Gunter, & Peterson, 1994). An introvert's brain must navigate through the teacher's expectations for class participation, the pressure to keep up with the chatty extroverts, the need to recall what another student has said, and yet still have enough brain power to process the original question posed by the teacher. The introvert then must divide her attention between the teacher, other students, and the material, while resisting any internal/external distractors, and act quickly in order to express herself in a discussion. Introverts understandably struggle with fast paced discussions. Instead, due to their strong long-term memory skills, they may do well delivering presentations that they have practiced multiple times instead of generating on-the-spot spontaneous comments.

Introverts also will likely to do better with self-reflective in-class assignments. Examples of such assignments that align with active learning practices include in-class writing reflections, "silent dialogue," and using clickers to answer questions (Weimer, 2013). In-class writing reflections require students to write thoughts and solutions to teacher-posed problems in class for at least ten minutes. A "silent dialogue" assignment asks students to write their answers or thoughts on a board in front of the classroom in a collaborative but primarily silent manner. Clickers can be used to ensure that all students can actively participate in the class without feeling on-the-spot, as most results of the answers are anonymous. These non-verbal assignments play to introverts' strengths of deep and meaningful reflection on the course material and allow introverts to participate actively without the pressure of speaking all the time. Silence in a classroom, except for on exam days, is an unusual and sometimes uncomfortable experience for students. However, even extroverts may benefit from taking time to self-reflect – as they have a tendency to react more impulsively than introverts (Matthews, 2009).

Collaborative learning. In general, groups are helpful for problem solving and thinking deeply due to common student behaviors of explaining, elaborating, and receiving feedback from other students (Weimer, 2013). Introverts want to feel connected to other students and the teacher; however, introverts do not feel this connection during lectures or large-group discussions. As introverts tend to prefer collaboration rather than argumentative discourse, they typically benefit from working together with another peer on a problem. Activities that foster learning in introverts are the Think-Pair-Share technique and small-group discussions, especially with a clear outcome or product post-discussion. In the Think-Pair-Share technique, students reflect independently on the question or problem, then pair with a partner to discuss their reflections, and then discuss these reflections with the large group. Even if introverts do not participate in the Share portion, they have engaged with their own thoughts and with another peer, which is synonymous with active learning. In small-group discussions, care should be taken to ensure that these discussions include a structured problem and that each student has a role within the small-group. Introverts may feel less overwhelmed in small-group environment with a select few students rather than a large group of students, thus encouraging them to participate. In this context, introverts may be able to make more substantial contributions than they would have in a large group, even if their contributions are still less frequent than extroverts.

Back to the personal story which began this essay. As an introvert, no matter how hard I tried, I could not match the frequent verbal comments of others because I am unable to change who I am. Over time, I have grown to accept that there is nothing negative about a personality. A personality just is. Quiet is a neutral term, not inherently negative, despite American's society's tendency to disparage shyness with non-synonyms as "backwards." Introversion is not a character flaw that has to be changed.

When I moved out of a deficit view of myself as an introverted person, I realized all the gifts that introversion gives me and others: thoughtful observations and insights, honest self-reflection, a calm presence, a love of writing, and ensuring others are listened to and heard. I am beginning to focus on my strengths by allowing myself time and space to process the material, rather than just pressuring myself to speak. However, as I am still a student approaching my last year of doctorate studies, situations often arise when I do need to participate in class for a grade. Sometimes, professors approach me to discuss any help I may need to participate verbally in class. I highly appreciate when professors do so and a discussion about my introversion or difficulties speaking up in class helps me feel more comfortable. The situations that are the most difficult for me are when professors assume that students who are struggling learn to advocate for themselves, which is no easy task.

My most recent stop in my learning journey involved approaching a professor after completing a written student information form that was distributed on the first day of class. On this student information form, I confided to the professor that I was an introvert. Taking this risk to share my introversion with the professor was difficult, but the response was enormously positive. Embedded in-class activities helped me engage with the material without feeling uncomfortable, because the professor provided options for pair and small group conversations, in groups of no more than 4 students. As an introvert, I do enjoy one-on-one and tiny group conversations. The Think-Pair-Share technique was my first introduction to active learning in a classroom context. I was excited that I could share my thoughts to one person without feeling overstimulated by class discussion. The "silent dialogue" technique was a new experience that allowed me to process material silently and use my strengths of writing. I felt connected to other students by reading their ideas on the board and felt more comfortable silently adding to the board rather than jumping into a discussion. In another class, I realized that an assignment that aligned with my goals included—gasp!—public speaking. When learning, mistakes are a given. For introverts, making mistakes is even more risky. However, learning is possible even for those of us who struggle to risk. We just need the right supports.

To support introverts, we need to shift the cultures of our

classrooms, beginning with a shift in understanding. The quiet students are told and encouraged to speak more frequently without regard to the effort and contributions of the few but meaningful comments they have made or the thoughtful questions they have posed. Does a classroom filled with heated discussion allow all students to learn effectively? It depends. Do tangential and personal stories that are only peripherally connected with the course material reflect thoughtful critical thinking? The key to answering such questions seems to be rethinking how student's best learn through in-depth reflection of course material. The scholarship of teaching and learning literature supports active learning, but active learning is more synonymous with "engagement" rather than "participation" (Cain & Klein, 2015). Introverts can show engagement. Yes, we may never enthusiastically jump into conversations. However, we may be processing the material at the very moment that another student has jumped into the conversation. And that, as the literature has shown, is learning.

References

Cain, S., & Klein, E. (2015). Engaging the quiet kids. *Independent School, 75*(1), 64–71. Retrieved from http://login.ezproxy.lib.umn.edu/login?url=http://search.ebscohost.com/login.aspx?direct=true&AuthType=ip,uid&db=aph&AN=109986387&site=ehost-live http://login.ezproxy.lib.umn.edu/login?url=http://search.ebscohost.com/login.aspx?direct=true&AuthType=ip,uid&db=aph&AN=109986387&site=ehost-live.

Carstens, B. A., Ciancio, D. J., Crabtree, K. E., Hart, L. A., Best, T. L., Trant, E. C., ... Williams, R. L. (2016). The effects of voluntary versus called-on participation on response rate in class discussion and performance on course exams. *Scholarship of Teaching and Learning in Psychology, 2*(3), 179–192. doi: http://dx.doi.org/10.1037/stl0000061http://dx.doi.org/10.1037/stl0000061 http://dx.doi.org/10.1037/stl0000061.

Dobbs, S., Furnham, A., & McClelland, A. (2011). The effect of background music and noise on the cognitive test performance of introverts and extraverts. *Applied Cognitive Psychology, 25*, 307–313. doi: 10.1002/acp.1692.

Furnham, A., Gunter, B., & Peterson, E. (1994). Television distraction and the performance of introverts and extroverts. *Applied Cognitive Psychology, 8(7)*, 705-711. doi: 10.1002/acp.2350080708.

Kennedy, P. (2002). Learning cultures and learning styles: myth-understandings about adult (Hong Kong) Chinese learners. *International Journal of Lifelong Education, 21(5)*, 430–445. doi: 10.1080/02601370210156745.

Lambert, C. (2003, July-August). Introversion unbound. *Harvard Magazine*. Retrieved from http://harvardmagazine.com/2003/07/introversion-unbound.htmlhttp://harvardmagazine.com/2003/07/introversion-unbound.html http://harvardmagazine.com/2003/07/introversion-unbound.html.

Markus, H. R., & Kitayama, S. (1991). Culture and the self: Implications for cognition, emotion, and motivation. *Psychological Review, 98*, 224-253. doi: 10.1037//0033-295X.98.2.2241037%2f%2f0033-295X.98.2.224.

Matthews, G. (2009). Personality and performance: cognitive processes and models. In P. J. Corr and G. Matthews (Eds.) *The Cambridge Handbook of Personality Psychology* (400-426). New York: Cambridge University Press.

Mueller, E. M., Burgdorf, C., Chavanon, M.-L., Schweiger, D., Wacker, J., & Stemmler, G. (2014). Dopamine modulates frontomedial failure processing of agentic introverts versus extraverts in incentive contexts. *Cognitive, Affective & Behavioral Neuroscience, 14*(2), 756–68. doi: 10.3758/s13415-013-0228-9.

Murray, H. G., & Lang, M. (1997). Does classroom participation improve student learning? *Society for Teaching and Learning in Higher Education, 20, 7-9*. Retrieved from http://www.stlhe.ca/wp-content/uploads/2011/07/Does-Classroom-Participation-Improve-Student-Learning.pdfhttp://www.stlhe.ca/wp-content/uploads/2011/07/Does-Classroom-Participation-Improve-Student-Learning.pdf.

Nussbaum, E. M. (2002). How introverts versus extroverts approach small-group argumentative discussions. *The Elementary School Journal, 102*, 183-197.

Pewewardy, C. (2002). Learning styles of American Indian/Alaska Native students: A review of the literature and implications for practice. *Journal of American Indian Education, 41*(3), 22-56. Retrieved from JSTOR.

Prince, M. (2004). Does active learning work? A review of the research. *Journal of Engineering Education, 93*(3), 223–232. doi: 10.1002/j.2168-9830.2004.tb00809.

Schmeck, R. R., & Lockhart, D. (1983). Introverts and extraverts require different learning environments. *Educational Leadership*, 54-55. Retrieved from PSYCInfo.

Smillie, L. D., Cooper, A. J., & Pickering, A. D. (2011). Individual differences in reward-prediction-error: extraversion and feedback-related negativity. *Social Cognitive and Affective Neuroscience, 6*(5), 646–652. doi: 10.1093/scan/nsq078.

Weimer, M. (2013). *Learner-centered teaching: Five key changes to practice*. San Francisco, CA: John Wiley & Sons.

Chapter Eight

Trigger Warnings in the Classroom

By Catherine Burke, Kaitlyn Hoitomt, Carson Haynes, & DeDe Wohlfarth

As we work to ensure that class content is relevant to students' everyday lives, some course material can be considered by student to be controversial, emotional challenging or difficult to discuss. This is particularly true when course topics connect with trauma, including sexual assault, race-based trauma, child abuse, and similar adverse experiences. Many students have experienced traumatic events in their lives, which disproportionally affect students of color and non-heterosexual students. As a result, students have requested, and many faculty have begun to use, trigger warnings to alert students that potentially difficult material is going to be presented or discussed. This chapter will discuss relevant research regarding the use of trigger warnings, particularly in regards to their effect on student motivation and learning.

Whatever the subject we teach, our content matter is made richer and more relevant by connecting it to students' everyday lives. Given the current high-charged social and political climate, making these connections has become fraught with challenges. One suggestion to navigate these challenges is the use of trigger warnings. A trigger warning is a brief caveat to students that the material they are about to be exposed to could be emotional, personally challenging, or upsetting and may "trigger" negative reactions (Rae, 2016). Although trigger warnings are a new phenomenon, educators and students have historically made their opinions known in academic contexts. The use of trigger warning is controversial, however. Some have argued that these warnings are compassionate ways to protect students from experiencing trauma reactions. Others have argued that they are simply another way for society to shield millennials from experiencing the painful reality of life (Essig, 2014).

Trigger warnings are particularly relevant to students of color. The reasons for this are manifold. First, students of color are more likely to have experienced traumatic events and adverse childhood experiences than their White colleagues (Boyraz, Horne, Armstrong, & Owens, 2015). Second, in our efforts to have open classroom dialogues around potentially difficult topics of racism, microaggressions, and privilege, students of color may face unique challenges to getting their voices heard (Sue, 2015). These two diverse topics, the prevalence of trauma in our society and the need to talk about racially related topics, have made our classrooms potential landmines. Navigating this difficult terrain has challenged professors to balance objectivity with opinions, support with confrontation, and good classroom etiquette with meaningful student learning. Trigger warnings have become the recommended solution to the uncharted terrain of this problem, but the research on their effectiveness is minimal. How is a professor to proceed in balancing these competing demands?

Objectives

This chapter will introduce the reader to the occurrence and impact of trauma on individuals, including the effect of trauma on brain functioning. Following this discussion, the controversy surrounding the use of trigger warnings in the classroom will be discussed so that readers may be better informed of both sides of the argument. A case study will then be presented and recommendations will be provided to help professors balance instructional needs while remaining sensitive to the impact of student exposure to potentially difficult material.

Literature Review
Prevalence of Trauma in College Students

Although this chapter specifically pertains to students in higher education, understanding the general neurological effects of trauma is an important backdrop. Traumatic events are defined as situations that threaten serious injury or death to one's self or others and induce feelings of horror, terror, or helplessness (APA, 2008). These negative experiences also affect one's ability to focus and concentrate, both vital skills in classroom learning.

One groundbreaking study on the enduring effects of trauma on children is known as "The ACE (Adverse Childhood Experiences) Study" (Felitti et al., 1998). This research involved studying more than 17,000 adults to better understand their childhood experiences, particularly negative events.

Researchers specifically asked participants about ten major areas, including emotional abuse, physical abuse, sexual abuse, emotional neglect, physical neglect, domestic violence where mother was the victim, substance abuse by a member of the household, mental illness of a household member, parental separation or divorce, and incarceration of a family member. The study demonstrated high positive correlations between these 10 adverse childhood experiences and current health and behavioral problems. As the number of adverse childhood experiences increased, the number of problems as an adult also increased. These problems included alcoholism, depression, suicide attempts, greater risk for intimate partner violence, substance abuse, medical diseases, and sexually transmitted diseases (Felitti et al., 1998).

Although tempting to dismiss the individuals who experienced such Adverse Childhood Experience to be rare and thus largely from our classrooms, epidemiological data suggests we should to otherwise. In other words, we should assume that many, if not most, of our students have experienced such traumatic life events. For example, one study conducted on an urban sample found that 65% of participants reported being victimized, while 98% of participants reported having witnessed violence (Rosenthal,

2000). Another study conducted on a rural sample found that approximately 80% of participants reported being victimized, while approximately 95% reported having witnessed violence (Scarpa, 2003). Between 39%-85% of children have witnessed community violence, while 66% have been directly victimized (APA, 2008). This data suggests that the majority of individuals in our society have been exposed to or victimized by violence.

With regards to the Adverse Childhood Experiences listed above, the data are also powerful regarding the widespread nature of such negative events. In a large community sample examining the prevalence of such experiences conducted by the American Psychological Association, over two thirds of participants reported experiencing a traumatic event by the age of 16 (APA, 2008). The study also found that adults who were sexually abused as children ranged from 25%–43%. This study suggests that roughly 1 in 4 or even 1 in 3 of the students sitting in our classrooms have experienced serious trauma, with sexual abuse being considered the "signature event" of Adverse Childhood Experiences.

Several studies specifically have examined the experience of trauma in college students (Gilin & Kaufman, 2015; Read, Ouimette, White, Colder, & Farrow, 2011; Smyth, Hockemeyer, Heron, Wonderlich, & Pennebaker, 2008). One study found that 66% of students had experienced a significant traumatic event in the past (Read et al., 20ll). This study also found that approximately 10% of college students surveyed met diagnostic criteria for Posttraumatic Stress Disorder (PTSD), a diagnostic category reflecting that the effects of trauma are affecting the person's day to day functioning (Read et al., 2011).

Another study with over 6,000 participants found similar results, providing more support for the prevalence of traumatic experiences in our students' backgrounds (Smythe et al., 2008). Smythe et al. found rates of trauma in college students between 55-84%, a strikingly high percentage that depended on gender, race, and socio-economic status in terms of one's specific risk. Nine percent of these students reported symptoms that met the threshold for PTSD (Smyth et. al, 2008). This data also suggests that more than half of the students in our classrooms have been affected by trauma. Taken together, these studies suggest that between one-third and one-half of college students have been affected by trauma.

In another study that focused on master's level social work students, researchers found that a large portion of the sample had also experienced trauma, as both witnesses and victims. Gilin and Kaufman (2015) found that more than half of the 162 students studied were trauma survivors. Additionally, over 50% of the sample had experienced parental separation or divorce, almost 40% experienced household substance abuse, and nearly 25% experienced household mental illness and emotional abuse. Twenty percent had survived sexual and physical abuse, and many others reported surviving childhood physical neglect and witnessing domestic violence. This study suggests that the prevalence of students who have survived trauma may be differentially affected by the students' selected course of study. For example, students who have survived trauma may be more drawn to fields like social work.

Prevalence of Trauma among Historically Marginalized Students

A relevant inquiry is answering how likely students of color are to experience traumatic events. A 2015 study (Boyraz et al., 2015) explored this issue by studying 930 college students, a sample which was approximately 2/3 African American students and 1/3 White students. Results showed that 74% of African American students and 68% of White students had experienced at least one traumatic event in their lifetime. The range of reported traumas for African-American students was slightly higher than the white students (1-10 vs. 1-8). These results suggest that a significant portion of college students of color may have survived traumatic experiences. Furthermore, Boyraz et al. found that gender and race affected overall depressive symptoms and overall perceptions of social support. More specifically, African American men were more likely to report witnessing or experiencing violence or losing a loved one to a violent death, while White men were more likely to endorse emotional abuse or neglect. Thus, traumatic experiences may affect students of color in different ways than White students.

Students who identify as sexual minorities also are at risk for having traumatic events in their past. A 2010 study compared incidents of exposure to trauma and the onset of PTSD in heterosexual individuals to LGB individuals (Roberts, Austin, Corliss, Vandermorris, & Koenen, 2010). Results found that those who identify as lesbian, bisexual, or gay had a greater overall risk of maltreatment in childhood, exposure to violence, and/or trauma to close friends or relatives than heterosexuals. Similarly, the risk of PTSD was higher among LGB participants as compared to those who identified as heterosexual.

Effects of Trauma Exposure on Classroom Functioning

Exposure to trauma can have significant impacts on functioning and education. Trauma symptoms can range in severity, but the horrific nature of the event is correlated with, but does not neatly predict, how severe a person's symptoms will be (APA, 2008). An individual can experience a range of traumatic responses and symptoms, yet not yet be diagnosed with full-blown PTSD, so it is helpful to think of traumatic reactions on a continuum. Common PTSD symptoms include flashbacks, or a re-experiencing of the traumatic event when triggered by a reminder of it, and nightmares of the event specifically or just bad nightmares in general. People with PTSD may also actively work to avoid any potential reminders of the event (triggers). They also may demonstrate hyperarousal, or feeing that they are constantly on "high alert" and expecting danger (APA, 2008).

These symptoms can affect a student's classroom performance. Because it takes a great deal of energy to remain in "high alert" status, students may have diminished concentration skills to attend to classroom material. They may also have flashbacks during class, as flashbacks are common when people "zone out," which, although we would like to believe otherwise, sometimes happens during our classrooms (APA, 2008).

Trauma can also lead to weaker social skills compared to peers with less adverse backgrounds, which can affect students as they work on small group projects (Crosby, 2015). Students with traumatic backgrounds are also more likely to have internal struggles to control their moods as well as external struggles to control their behavior. Crosby (2015) found that students with trauma backgrounds tend to have lower grade point averages, test scores, and decreased academic performances compared to their peers.

Trigger Warnings

Given the high prevalence of traumatization of college students and awareness of the effects of trauma, advocates have suggested that professors use trigger warnings as a tool to alert students that potentially difficult classroom material will be discussed (Boysen, Wells, & Dawson, 2016). The use of trigger warnings was predominately student-driven and the rationale for such warnings was that students with traumatic backgrounds need to have the opportunity to mentally prepare themselves for classroom material that may serve as a reminder to the trauma they have experienced. The acceptance of trigger warnings by higher education has been uneven, contributing to some level of polarization between students and faculty. Although students generally have advocated for the use of trigger warnings, some professors have dismissed them as barriers to student learning and growth (Essig, 2014; Rae, 2016).

The argument against the use of trigger warnings is that higher education is designed to challenge students' worldviews and provide opportunities to students to recognize that their worldview is not universal. This paradigm shift helps students create cognitive, personal, and emotional connections with new ideas, values, and others (Gubkin, 2015). Such exposure to difficult material is vital to create growth and learning. Some educators assert that trigger warnings deprive students of the opportunity to be exposed the unsettled feelings that often precede learning (Rae, 2016).

One major concern is that trigger warnings will reduce a rich and complex work into a single label, thereby dismissing the intricacy of the work (Crosby, 2015). For example, a book that contains a suicide as a minor part of the story may receive a "suicide warning" label, which may dissuade students from reading the book. For example, *The Great Gatsby* could receive trigger warnings of domestic abuse and graphic violence. Some professors argue that reducing a great literary work to a trigger warning is a superficial approach to engaging with a classic creation. As one professor said, "The presumption there is that students should not be forced to deal with something that makes them uncomfortable is absurd or even dangerous" (Flood, 2014). A fear voiced by some professors related to this idea is that students who have received trigger warnings will choose not to attend class the day that the material is being shown, read, or discussed (Flaherty, 2015). If students are refusing to engage with material based on trigger warnings, instructors argue, the warnings are more problematic than helpful.

On the other hand, some of the research on trigger warnings has shown that some professors fear using them out of compassionate concern for student reactions (Flaherty, 2015). Specifically, some professors fear that issuing a trigger warning may have a priming effect on students, inadvertently leading students to prepare for a stressful experience that would not have otherwise experienced (Flaherty, 2015).

Some students, and professors as well, argue that trigger warnings are helpful (Flaherty, 2015). They argue that without them, traumatic responses can become so overwhelming that the student cannot interact with the material at all, thus rendering the student unable to learn. The pro-trigger warning group has pushed for trigger warnings to be institutionally required across classes. These proponents argue that trigger warnings are not only humane, but necessary, given the high rates of students with adverse backgrounds (Flaherty, 2015). Providing a safe space for students to explore their reactions to the material is suggested as a crucial step toward academic compassion, trust, and enlightenment (Flaherty, 2015).

In finding a balance between these positions, Godderis and Root (2016) suggest the use of student feedback to help professors decide how to best use trigger warnings in their classes. Godderis and Root recognize the concerns of refuters as including threatening academic freedom as well as infantilizing students by shielding them from the realworld. However, Godderis and Root argue that these beliefs emanate from a misunderstanding of trigger warnings. Specifically, they argue that this perspective operates from a misassumption that college students have yet to experience the real world. However, trigger warnings are an acknowledgement of students who have experienced trauma of the real world. Godderis and Root also argue that trigger warnings give more autonomy and offer empathy, respect, and consent to students who have experienced the "real world." This stance takes a considerate approach in which both instructors and students can have their needs met in the academic environment.

Case Study

A'kierra is a first year 19-year-old African American, cisgender female student at a large Midwestern university. During her sophomore year in high school, she was date raped by a high school acquaintance. After therapy, A'kierra struggled with sleeplessness due to nightmares. In the daytime, she had flashbacks of the event. Despite attending therapy since high school, A'kierra continues to struggle with managing her traumatic symptoms.

During A'kierra's first semester, she enrolled in an introductory film class in which the professor showed Last Tango in Paris. The film contains an explicit and violent scene where a young woman is raped by an acquaintance. The instructor gave no warning before the film and A'kierra began to hyperventilate in class. She rushed out of class in the middle of the film and never returned to the class. For the next week, A'kierra suffered from increased nightmares and flashbacks. She never told her professor about why she suddenly left the class.

A'kierra is also taking a required English literature course. Her professor has assigned reading a text that graphically explores the rape of a young woman. At the beginning of the course, A'kierra's instructor discussed the concept of trauma and relayed to the students that the material covered in the course may be upsetting, but that an emotional reaction was helpful in understanding key literature devices, such as perspective taking and character development. Her English professor provided the phone number to the university counseling center in the syllabus. The week prior to a class discussion on the book, A'kierra's instructor again reminded students that they would be discussing the material the following week and to ensure that they took care of themselves before, during, and after reading it. A'kierra met with her therapist to discuss the book, and although the reading was difficult for her, she was able to manage her emotional reactions to the material so she could learn.

Recommendations

The following recommendations may be helpful in creating a classroom that is supportive of students with traumatic backgrounds while still allowing students to interact with controversial or sensitive material.

1. Despite the inherent ambiguity and challenges in learning, professors should strive to create classroom cultures of inclusion and empathy (Crosby, 2015). Although impossible to determine one "right" answer regarding how to manage students' emotional reactions (Abrams & Shapiro, 2014), building trust between professors and students is certainly helpful. Professors help students by openly discussing how class content may be difficult, but that it is valuable in helping students understand the world (Parrenas, 2014). Some educators have found it useful to discuss the potential for growth after trauma and incorporate that information into their classrooms (Gilin & Kaufman,

2015). Professors are also encouraged to describe the difficult content of the material, share its historical context, and explain why it is valuable to understanding class content (Gubkin, 2015).
2. Boysen, Wells and Dawson (2016) recommend providing both written trigger warnings in the syllabus, as well as verbal trigger warnings in the classroom. Currently, approximately 72% of faculty surveyed provide verbal trigger warnings, whereas only 37% provide written warnings in the syllabus (Boysen, Wells, & Dawson, 2016). Providing contact information for the university counseling center in the syllabus is also recommended.
3. Although students may emotionally struggle to read or discuss difficult material, avoiding reminders of the traumatic event is a common symptom of PTSD. However, avoiding exposure to traumatic events allows trauma responses to continue (Roff, 2014). Stringer (2016) and Crosby (2015) suggest using trigger warnings as a forecasting of upcoming events rather than removing sensitive content from course content. Stringer avers that students should be required to consume all mandatory course materials but in an inclusive and compassionate environment with clear, but supportive expectations (Crosby, 2015). Grubkin (2015) adds that incorporating emotions into learning experiences enriches students' deep learning.
4. Showing sensitive material in the beginning of the class and leaving time for students to discuss their reactions is helpful (Stringer, 2016). Similarly, allowing students to utilize personal journals to process their reactions privately can be beneficial (Gilin & Kaufman, 2015).
5. Educators should strive to be aware of their cultural biases and assumptions, so they can manage these biases in the classroom (Crosby, 2015). Professors may or may not have their own experiences with trauma, but every-

one's response to trauma is different. Every response should be treated with respect and dignity.

6. If professors have created a supportive classroom culture, students may approach the professor to share their own personal traumas. If this happens, professors should be empathic and compassionate, but be careful not to create a dual relationship with students by trying to serve as therapists as well as professors (Crosby, 2015; Cunningham, 2004). A sensitive referral to the university counseling center is the best approach in these situations. Maintaining the students' confidentiality (Abrams & Shapiro, 2014) is also paramount.

References

Abrams, J. & Shapiro, M. (2014). Teaching trauma theory and practice in MSW programs: A clinically focused, case based method. *Clinical Social Work Journal, 42,* 408- 418.

American Psychological Association (APA) Presidential Task Force on Posttraumatic Stress Disorder and Trauma in Children and Adolescents (2008). *Children and trauma: Update for mental health professionals.* American Psychological Association. Washington DC. Retrieved from http://www.apa.org/pi/families/resources/children-trauma-update.aspx.

Boyraz, G., Horne, S. G., Armstrong, A. P., & Owens, A. C. (2015). Posttraumatic stress predicting depression and social support among college students: Moderating effects of race and gender. *Psychological Trauma: Theory, Research, Practice, And Policy, 7*(3), 259-268.

Boysen, G.A., Wells, A.M., & Dawson, K.J. (2016). Instructors' use of trigger warnings and behavior warnings in abnormal psychology. *Teaching of Psychology, 43*(4), 334-339.

Crosby, S.D. (2015). An Ecological perspective on emerging trauma informed teaching practices. *Children & Schools, 37*(4), 223- 230.

Cunningham, M. (2004). Teaching social workers about trauma: Reducing the risks of vicarious trauma in the classroom. *Journal of Social Work Education, 40*(2), 305-317.

Essig, L. (2014). Trigger warnings trigger me. *The Chronicle of Higher Education, 60*(27), B2

Felitti, V.J., Anda, R.F., Nordenberg, D., Williamson, D.F., Spitz, A.M., Edwards,V., & Koss, M.P. (1998). The relationship of adult health status to childhood abuse and household dysfunction. *American Journal of Preventive Medicine, 14,* 245- 258.

Flaherty, C. (2015, December 3). The never-ending trigger-warning debate. Retrieved from http://www.slate.com/articles/life/inside_higher_ed/2015/12/trigger_warning_debate_some_professors_say_they_build_trust_others_say_they.html.

Flood, A. (2014, May 19). US students request trigger warnings on literature. Retrieved from https://www.theguardian.com/books/2014/may/19/us-students-request-trigger warnings-in-literature.

Gilin, B. & Kauffman, S. (2015). Strategies for teaching about trauma to graduate social work students. *Journal of Teaching in Social Work, 35*, 378–396.

Godderis, R., & Root, J. L. (2016). Trigger warnings: Compassion is not censorship. *Radical Pedagogy, 13*(2), 130-138.

Gubkin, L. (2015). From empathetic understanding to engaged witnessing: Encountering trauma in the holocaust classroom. *Teaching Theology and Religion, 18*(2), 103-120.

Parrenas, J. (2014). Why trigger warnings harm instead of help. *Lesbian News, 39* (11), 20.

Rae, L. (2016). Re-focusing the debate on trigger warnings: Privilege, trauma, and disability in the classroom. *First Amendment Studies, 5 0*(2), 95-102.

Read, J. P., Ouimette, P., White, J., Colder, C., & Farrow, S. (2011). Rates of DSM–IV–TR trauma exposure and posttraumatic stress disorder among newly matriculated college students. *Psychological Trauma: Theory, Research, Practice, And Policy, 3*(2), 148-156.

Roberts, A. L., Austin, S. B., Corliss, H. L., Vandermorris, A. K., & Koenen, K. C. (2010). Pervasive Trauma Exposure among US Sexual Orientation Minority Adults and Risk of Posttraumatic Stress Disorder. *American Journal of Public Health, 100*(12), 2433-2441.

Roff, S. (2014). Treatment, not "trigger warnings." *Chronicle of Higher Education, 60*(38).

Rosenthal, B.S. (2000). Exposure to community violence in adolescence: Trauma symptoms. *Adolescence, 35*(138), 271-284.

Scarpa, A. (2003). Community violence exposure in young adults. *Trauma Violence Abuse, 4*(3), 210-227.

Smyth, J.M., Hockemeyer, J.R., Heron, K.E., Wonderlich, S.A., & Pennebaker, J.W. (2008). Prevalence, type, disclosure, and severity of adverse life events in college students. *Journal of American College Health, 57*(1), 69-76.

Stringer, R. (2016). Reflection from the field. *Women's Studies Journal, 30*(2), 62-66.

Sue, D.W. (2015). *Race talks and the conspiracy of silence.* Hoboken, NJ: John Wiley and Sons.

Chapter Nine
Responding To Gender and Sexual Identity Diversity in the College Classroom

By Tara M. Tuttle

This chapter will discuss how to reconceptualize the college classroom in ways that better serve LGBTQIA students. Instructors must develop a working knowledge of both gender identity and sexual orientation in order to respond effectively to gender and sexual identity diversity in the classroom. Even those aware of gender and sexual identity diversity and those committed to the rights of LGBTQIA individuals may teach in ways that unwittingly reinforce gender and sexual identity hierarchies and further marginalize LGBTQIA students. To respond with cultural competence to LGBTQIA students, instructors must build trust with LGBTQIA students through acknowledgment, affirmation, and inclusion.

Instructors must develop a working knowledge of both gender identity and sexual orientation in order to respond effectively to gender and sexual identity diversity in the classroom. Gender identity is a person's perception of their own gender, while sexual orientation is one's sexual identity based on one's patterns of sexual and/or romantic attractions. Misconceptions about these concepts are common, even in the ostensibly progressive halls of academe. I have worked with professors who did not know what *any* of the letters in the abbreviation LGBTQIA stands for; more common is awareness of the first four or five letters (which stand for lesbian, gay, bisexual, transgender, and queer) with questions on the I (intersex) and A (asexual, not "ally" as is commonly assumed). Still, knowing what identities to which those letters refer is not an indicator that instructors know much about those identities or how to respond to students who possess them. Even those well aware of gender and sexual identity diversity and even those fully committed to the rights of LGBTQIA individuals often teach in ways that unwittingly reinforce gender and sexual identity hierarchies or in ways that further marginalize LGBTQIA students.

In *Border Crossing: Cultural Workers and the Politics of Education,* Giroux (1992) points out how this happens. He writes, "The first question is: Can learning take place if in fact it silences the voices of people it is supposed to teach? And the answer is: Yes. People learn that they don't count" (p. 16). LGBTQIA students have learned they don't count in most classrooms. Spiegel (2011) writes, "we cannot deny and divest youth of their sexualities, their sexual desire and agency, and more importantly that they bring all of that into the classroom. This [stated preconception] also affects how we have conceptualized the classroom, as based in a mind/body split" (p. 23). We must reconceptualize the classroom in ways that better serve LGBTQIA students. Meyer (2012) insists, "Educators need to have accurate information and support to educate their students and communities around issues of gender, sex, and sexuality and how discrimination based on any of these ground harms everyone in schools. By developing a more critical understanding of these issues, educators can have a profound impact on the way students learn, relate to others, and behave in schools" (p. 10).

Even when homophobia—prejudice against LGBTQIA persons—is not overt in their courses, affirmation of LGBTQIA viewpoints rarely is. Professors and students who may feel strongly that they are not homophobic may still be heterosexist. Heterosexism is bias in favor of heterosexual practices and the attitudes that derive from viewing heterosexuality as the norm for relationships or sexual activity. While homophobia is often more overt in its discriminatory manifestations against LGBTQIA individuals, heterosexism also marginalizes LGBTQIA persons in the many ways it promotes the privileging of heterosexual persons and experiences. Understanding this distinction is crucial to creating inclusive environments for LGBTQIA persons. It is also important to note that even LGBTQIA persons frequently internalize homophobic and heterosexist cultural messages and that even LGBTQIA instructors and students may contribute to the marginalization of LGBTQIA persons in higher education. Finally, though this article addresses issues faced by LGBTQIA students, one must always be mindful of the ways in which other factors of identity shape their experiences of oppression. LGBTQIA students do not necessarily share similar experiences in our classrooms or in their cultures. Race, ethnicity, socioeconomic status, religion, age, ability, citizenship, gender, region, and other factors will contribute to the experiences and positions of LGBTQIA persons in higher education and other realms.

To be culturally competent is to know about diverse identities and be able to respond to difference effectively, but it would be incompetent to assume all members of certain gender or sexual identity groups share similar attributes or experiences. While it is crucial to note gender identity and sexual orientation variance does exist in the classroom, it is equally crucial to avoid perpetuating problematic stereotypes about gender identity and sexual orientation. Instructors must share with Spiegel (2011) the commitment to "make[ing] sure that [her] students are aware not to tokenize—that there are many different kinds of queer individuals, just as there are many different kinds of heterosexual individuals" (p. 25). As Johnson III and Rivera (2015) rightly state, "the best classroom experiences bring all students, majority and minority alike, to increased biocognitive ability, or greater context diversity (Ibarra, 2001), and therefore to the possibility of greater mutual appreciation" (p. 512). This article is intended for those unfamiliar with contemporary understandings of gender and sexuality and strives to bring its audience into greater appreciation of gender and sexual identity diversity.

Some instructors claim these issues do not pertain to their

classes if they teach subjects that seem neutral or abstract in relation to personal experience—physics or math, for example. However, education is a fundamentally human enterprise; even those instructors whose content does not deal directly with the human experience cannot claim to inhabit classrooms in which gender identity and sexual orientation do not matter. Classroom interactions themselves are shaped by understandings (and misunderstandings) of gender and sexual identity. When a professor believes they treat all students the same way without understanding that all students don't receive that treatment in the same way, they often believe they are operating with a neutrality that does not in reality exist.

Mufioz-Plaza, Quinn, and Rounds (2002) describe the classroom as "the most homophobic of all social institutions" (p. 53). Whether or not we agree with such a provocative assertion, we must be deliberate in our endeavor to ensure it does not accurately describe our own classrooms. Using Connolly's (2000) continuum of classroom experiences to frame my discussion, in this article I will offer methods for moving from the explicit marginalization LGBTQIA students often face in college courses toward attainment of the goal of explicit centralization necessary for full inclusion of and effective response to LGBTQIA students. Connolly (2000) describes four stages of LGBTQIA experience in the classroom: explicit marginalization, implicit marginalization, implicit centralization, and explicit centralization. In a classroom in which LGBTQIA students are explicitly marginalized, heterosexist and homophobic remarks are present and uncontested in classroom discussion via the instructor or students or in class readings (p. 114). In a classroom in which LGBTQIA students experience implicit marginalization, heterosexist and homophobic remarks may be subtle while the perspectives of LGBTQIA individuals are rendered invisible through exclusion (p. 116). In a classroom in which LGBTQIA students experience implicit centralization, positive messages about LGBTQIA persons may be articulated by the professor, in instructional materials, or from students, and homophobic and heterosexist remarks may be resisted by the professor or students; however, the validation of LGBTQIA persons is intermittent and spontaneous rather than due to deliberately inclusive pedagogy (p. 119). For full inclusion of LGBTQIA students, a classroom experience of explicit centralization is best. In a classroom in which LGBTQIA students are explicitly centralized, the instructor clearly articulates the message that not only is homophobia and heterosexism impermissible in this class, but also that the perspectives of LGBTQIA persons are crucial to the course and of equal value to those of heterosexual persons (p. 120). In the following five sections, I provide basic information and offer suggestions for centralizing LGBTQIA students in the classroom. These include knowing the basic terminology and concepts, adopting an inclusive curriculum, using inclusive language and examples, inviting students to share but not to represent, and deconstructing heterosexuality and cisgenderism.

I. Know the Basics

The initial problem to be surmounted is the knowledge gap among instructors concerning issues of gender identity and sexual diversity. The full complexity of these concepts is not widely understood outside of the field of Gender Studies, yet they shape classroom dynamics in every discipline, and every discipline has faculty and students who identify as LGBTQIA and/or nonbinary (defined below). One could not redress this knowledge gap in a single article, and I will not attempt to do so here, but some basic concepts are crucial to understanding how and why cultural competencies in gender identity and sexual orientation must be attained by contemporary educators.

Gender is not biology. Though both our understandings of sex and gender are socially constructed and not prone to accurate simple reduction, sex refers to the classification of male or female based upon physiological characteristics of genital anatomy and/or chromosomal makeup. In contrast, gender is the complex array of social and cultural attributes and roles linked to beliefs about the two sexes. Even sex, though, is more complex than many would like to admit when we consider that up to 1.7% of individuals do not fit the sex binary classification system and are intersex, a term which describes a person born with reproductive anatomy, chromosomal makeup, or sex hormone levels that do not neatly match that which is considered typical for a male or female body (Free & Equal: United Nations for LGBT Equality, 2015). Consideration of how many individuals exist outside the sex binary reveals its limits.

A gender binary, then, is even less fixed. When we talk about a gender binary, we mean the artificial classification of attributes commonly ascribed to gender into two distinct categories, masculine and feminine, which are often (mis)understood as opposites. A quick inspection of any classroom at a U.S. public institution today reveals numerous ways of doing gender, or of being a gendered person. Humans of any gender exhibit a variety of traits and behaviors, some of which are considered traditionally masculine and some of which are considered traditionally feminine. For example, a person who identifies as a woman, whose sex assigned at birth was female, and who may appear conventionally feminine in numerous ways may still possess some traits considered traditionally masculine such as assertiveness, athleticism, competitiveness, or even physical strength. Neither one's gender nor one's anatomy restricts the possibilities for possessing traits affiliated with a different gender. Nevertheless, binary thinking about gender persists in ways that contribute to misapprehensions of gender and sexual identity and discrimination. Binary thinking about gender remains popular despite many examples of its invalidity.

Gender identity is one's perception of one's own gender, which may or may not correspond to the sex one was assigned at birth. These, too, are shaped by the coercive forces of sexism and heterosexism, though individuals may resist such coercion. One's gender identity may evolve over time. According to Agid and Rand (2011), "gender expressions and identities are brought into line with gender assignments through the workings of intimate and large-scale forces involved in policing, reward, and surveillance—always in ways shaped by sexuality, race, ethnicity, class, economic situation, nationality, and relation to the state, whether documented or undocumented" (p. 7). Gender identity, shaped by these other aspects of identity and status, is related to one's gender expression, which refers to how one presents one's gender identity in external appearance.

The term "cisgender" is an adjective referring to a person whose gender identity corresponds to their sex assigned at birth. "Transgender" is an adjective referring to a person whose gender identity does not align with their sex assigned at birth. Individuals who are transgender (sometimes referred to simply as "trans") or who are in the process of transitioning may make choices about hair, clothing, comportment, behavior, voice, cosmetic use, hormone therapy, name and pronoun use, and other practices in order to more closely align their gender expression to their gender identity. Transgender persons may or may not elect to undergo sex reassignment surgery, which is not a requirement for a trans identity.

The term "nonbinary" refers to a person whose gender identity and gender expression do not adhere to either the traditionally masculine or feminine options to which the gender binary limits us. Sometimes, nonbinary and trans individuals are actively striving to deconstruct the gender binary in recognition of the ways it contributes to gender-based oppression.

Sexual identity, also referred to as sexual orientation, is based on one's patterns of sexual and/or romantic attractions. Though many labels for the wide varieties of sexual orientations exist, common options include heterosexual (straight), homosexual (lesbian or gay), bisexual, or pansexual/polysexual. The term "bisexual" was previously understood as referring to a person who may experience romantic or sexual attractions to either same or opposite gender persons; however, many now understand the term "bisexual" to be similar in meaning to the labels "pansexual" and "polysexual" which refer to a person who may experience romantic or sexual attractions to persons of any gender. (The latter are distinct from the former in its recognition of the fact that the term "bisexuality" reinforces the gender binary.) Though previously used as a slur, the word "queer" has been reclaimed as an umbrella term for any non-heterosexual sexual orientation or for those who reject traditional notions of gender and sexuality in their relationship practices and/or gender expressions. Meyer (2012) writes, "'Queer' is understood as a challenge to traditional understandings of sexual identity that deconstructs the categories, binaries, and language that supports them" (p. 13-14). For some, though, the word still carries its derogatory connotations; instructors must be sensitive to this. The term's popularity among academic circles may be entirely unknown to many students, and some LGBTQIA students may find its use offensive. Discussion of the term's history is recommended upon the introduction of this term in a classroom setting.

Similar to the term "heterosexism" defined above, heteronormativity is the reinforcement of heterosexuality through coercive cultural messages that cast heterosexuality as the norm and preferred way of practicing sexuality and relationships. According to Blackburn and Smith (2010), "When understood as normal, straightness escapes criticism and as such takes on invisibility, thus positioning all other orientations as abnormal or deviant. Just as straightness-as-normal is problematic, heteronormativity, too, is a faulty premise" (p. 626-627). The heteronormativity of a culture is exhibited via a wide variety of messages and practices including but not limited to tax codes, employment benefits, adoption policies, school dress codes, extracurricular activities, childrearing practices, complementarian religious understandings of gender, and media representations that favor straight persons and couples and which may deliberately or unintentionally exclude LGBTQIA persons or same-sex couples. When we acknowledge the pervasiveness of cultural messages promoting heterosexuality, we see clearly that heterosexuality is not strictly a biological impulse but a learned behavior reinforced through thousands of coercive cultural practices.

For most instructors and students, though, gender and sexuality are concepts they live out uncritically, perhaps nearly unconsciously after decades of socialization. Meyer (2012) explains, "The invisible nature of gender socialization contributes to its strength and illustrates how hegemony works" (p. 10). What role in this manufactured invisibility of gender and sexual identity norms does an educational institution play? "Schools also frequently and actively silence any discourse that could be seen as positive toward gender and sexual diversity through the official and hidden curriculum," Meyer (2012) points out, which must "[lead] us into a discussion of how the use of language and activities of surveillance in schools contribute to creating school climates that are hostile to gender and sexual diversity and reinforce the supremacy of heterosexuality" (p. 11).

Analogous to the concept of heteronormativity is the concept of cisnormativity. "Cisnormativity" refers to the discriminatory assumption that all humans are cisgender, the ways in which transgender and nonbinary experiences are rendered invisible among cultural practices and representations, and the coercive social, political, and religious messages that encourage cisgender identity and discourage transgender identity.

If instructors are unaware of these concepts and/or unwilling to address these issues, they will perpetuate discrimination against LGBTQIA students in their classrooms. Both instructors and "students are indoctrinated with the understanding that gender and, implicitly, attractions are both denoted and inescapably determined by one's genitalia. If this understanding is in place, then it is no wonder that students and teachers have trouble imagining anything but a traditional gender binary related to heterosexual desires in formalized school spaces" (Blackburn & Smith, 2010, p. 627). Knowledge about gender and sexual identity diversity gives us the power to change this, as does a deliberate, liberatory pedagogy that explicitly centralizes LGBTQIA experience.

II. Adopt an Inclusive Curriculum

To move beyond explicit and implicit marginalization toward explicit centralization, instructors must incorporate LGBTQIA perspectives into the curriculum. Reece-Miller (2010) points out, "The curriculum in American schools is by and large founded on heterosexism and continues to exclude LGTBQ content" (p. 74).

Using an inclusive curriculum makes a significant difference in the lives of LGBTQIA students. According to the GLSEN 2015 National Climate Survey Executive Summary, "75.2% of LGBTQ students in schools with an inclusive curriculum said their peers were accepting of LGBTQ people, compared to 39.6% of those without an inclusive curriculum" (8). That constitutes a considerable gap and a clear way to improve the experiences of LGBTQIA students.

Members of non-normative identities are already accustomed to having their experiences ignored or even stigmatized in the classroom. Educators must work to disrupt the expectation of marginalization that students with non-normative gender and sexual identities may hold. In order to disrupt this expectation, educators must be sufficiently informed about gender and sexual identity and must be committed to egalitarian pedagogy that ends its perpetuation in the classroom. For those outside the interdiscipline of Gender Studies, this might mean educating oneself on the social construction of gender and sexuality, the gender binary, sexual fluidity, and the ways in which patriarchal and heteronormative educational practices have reinforced inequality.

III. Use Inclusive Language and Examples

Diversifying the curriculum is admittedly easier in some disciplines than others, but one simple action all instructors can immediately implement is the use of inclusive language. Something as simple as adopting the use of the singular "they" can facilitate the creation of a more inclusive environment. Though the use of the singular "they" prompts some resistance from those who favor strict adherence to rules of grammar, instructors likely already use this construction with regularity. ("Oh no, someone forgot their umbrella. I hope they come back to get it!") Shifting to the use of the singular "they" avoids reification of the gender binary inherent in "he or she" constructions. Instructors can deliberately incorporate examples using the singular "they" instead of or in addition to sentences in which they would use "he" or "she" separately or together. Such moves are likely to be appreciated by nonbinary individuals in the class who may feel acknowledged and welcomed by instructor recognition of the use of "they/them/their" pronouns. In order to avoid tripping over such constructions in class, which will only augment the sense that gender nonconforming and nonbinary students are excluded from the norm, I suggest instructors unfamiliar with this practice rehearse such examples until they flow smoothly prior to incorporating them into classroom use.

The use of "his or her" in the classroom not only reinforces the gender binary, it can result in misgendering one's students. "Misgendering" is the act of calling a person by pronouns that they do not use or which do not match their gender identity. It may also violate the current understanding of Title IX, the federal law ensuring equity in education regardless of gender. Though a February 2017 "Dear Colleague Letter" issued by the Department of Education Office of Civil Rights rescinded the Obama administration's May 13, 2016 "Dear Colleague Letter on Transgender Students" which had extended the understanding of Title IX's language on gender to include protections for transgender students, multiple circuit courts, the Equal Employment Opportunity Commission and the Department of Health and Human Services have all ruled that discrimination against persons on the basis of transgender identity violates existing laws outlawing gender-based discrimination (Holloway, 1977; Oncale, 1998; Smith, 2004; Glenn, 2011; EEOC, 2012; Office of the Federal Register, 2016). What rights will be guarded for transgender students in educational institutions remains to be seen, though many colleges and universities extend protections for these students in their own nondiscrimination policies. Regardless of written policy and law, however, is the simple concern for respect. Respecting a student's pronouns and gender identity is the only appropriate course of action to demonstrate cultural competency with gender and sexual diversity.

Some instructors call attention to pronoun use through syllabus statements, classroom discussions, and email signatures. The instructor may mention their own pronouns and invite students to share the pronouns they would like the instructor to use for them. Instructors should also be aware that in addition to the familiar he/him/his and she/her/hers pronouns are not only the use of they/them/theirs but gender neutral alternatives including ne/nim/nir/nirs, ve/ver/vis, ze/hir/hirs, xe/xem/xyr/xyrs, and ey/em/eir/eirs. Asking about pronouns may feel strange initially, but it is no harder than adding a short statement to one's introduction in the first class. For example, in classes, I say, "I'm Dr. Tuttle and my pronouns are she, her, and hers. Please let me know how you'd like me to address you." Other instructors have students identify their pronouns as part of the first in-class quiz or assignment. Avoid assuming you can judge by students' appearances the pronouns students would like you to use.

IV. Invite Students to Share But Do Not Ask Them to Represent

Instructors should never make assumptions about students' gender or sexual identities, and instructors should never call on a student because of their perceived identity to require them to speak on behalf of a particular identity group in class. Asking a student to represent an entire identity group can have the effect of explicit marginalization, casting them as "other" and of presenting the experiences of a minority group as homogenous. Johnston (1995) explains, "Stereotypes based on totalizing identities are not dismantled by presenting individuals as representative of an identity group, even if the participants are chosen to confirm the humanity of their group" (p. 116). Traditional college-aged students today are increasingly resistant to the labeling of identities and more comfortable with ambiguity, fluidity, and non-binary understandings of gender and sexuality. One also risks the violence of outing if calling on a student to share insights of LGBTQIA experience. Even if a student has shared information with you in course assignments, it is important to understand that people may be out to some individuals and not out to others, or that disclosing information in a classroom setting could potentially endanger them by exposing them to those who might harass, reject, or condemn them. On the other hand, if students wish to voluntarily share their perspectives as positioned within those identities, creating space for the inclusion of those narratives can help democratize the course experience and increase cultural competency. To empower students and increase agency, particularly among those likely to be explicitly and implicitly marginalized in educational settings, instructor practices must ensure that students have the choice to disclose personal experience and have control over their gender and sexual identities in the classroom.

V. Deconstruct Heterosexuality and Cisgenderism

Understand that tolerance for any minority group is an inadequate pedagogical goal. Instructors who wish to exhibit cultural competency must create an affirmative, not merely tolerant classroom environment. Moving beyond tolerance to competency requires a more sophisticated comprehension of the ways in which gender and sexuality are cultural constructions. Competency requires instructors to refrain from allowing heterosexuality and cisgender identity to persist as neutral, unquestioned defaults with which LGBTQIA experiences are contrasted, or even compared. Once instructors have mastered these basic tenets, another way to realize the goal of explicit centralization of LGBTQIA students is to deconstruct heterosexual and cisgender identities in the classroom. Doing so will help students see identities that they may see normal (heterosexuality and cisgenderism) are also socially constructed, culturally situated concepts and practices which are not static but have changed dramatically over time.

To simply defend LGBTQIA persons is insufficient. G. D. Shlasko (2005) explains, "we do not tell [students] that it is okay to be heterosexual. The very pronouncement of tolerance assumes an underlying intolerance; to say it is okay to be gay or lesbian assumes that, although 'okay,' it is not normal or desirable. Furthermore, simply to tell students that they are okay belies the lived experiences of queer kids who feel themselves violently excluded from the realm of normal. They know very well that something is not okay" (p. 126). This result is inevitable unless we learn to frame the discussions of gender and sexual identity as ones involving the power dynamics of normalcy from the start.

The ineffectiveness of approaches that avoid disruption of the binary is why feminist theorists take issue with the add-minority-voices-and-stir approach to inclusion. Winans (2006) believes that "Without beginning discussions by focusing explicitly on heterosexuality and how it is constructed and supported, gay identity would likely remain the only visible and socially constructed category for most students" (p. 111). Many students and instructors are mired in binary thinking about sex and gender, and this can prevent analysis of LGBTQIA persons and experiences from doing much other than revealing homophobia and increasing tolerance for the "other," demystifying the difference but not deconstructing the dichotomy. Britzman (1998) identifies this problem in her oft-cited essay "Is There a Queer Pedagogy? Or, Stop Reading Straight." She explains, "In an odd turn of events, curricula that proport to be inclusive may actually work to produce new forms of exclusivity *if* the only subject positions offered are the tolerant normal and the tolerated subaltern" (p. 221).

An approach that moves beyond merely defending LGTBQIA students against homophobia and heterosexism to deconstructing heterosexuality and cisgender identity does not simply help students better understand issues of gender and sexual identity but also the nature of knowledge construction. Winans (2006) explains, "In discussing sexual difference in class, then, students ask themselves questions like these: How do I feel and what do I know about this topic? Where does my knowledge come from? What is unknown to me? What is unthinkable to me and why? Questions like these are central to queer pedagogy because they help students learn both *that* knowledge is created and *how* knowledge is created" (p. 105). This is a crucial development in achieving the goals of a liberal arts education, and an urgently needed skill in the current climate in which the deliberate widespread dissemination of misinformation is intended to manipulate social and political outcomes.

Those of us who embrace these pedagogical practices have

admittedly lofty goals. Meyer (2012) writes, "In calling on educators to question and reformulate through a queer pedagogical lens (1) how they teach and reinforce gendered practices in schools, (2) how they support traditional notions of heterosexuality, and (3) how they present culturally specific information in the classroom, we will be able to reduce and eventually remove gendered harassment and other related forms of discrimination from schools, and consequently most realms of society" (p. 15). Regardless of our disciplines, those of us interested in social justice in higher education and in demonstrating cultural competency in the classroom should never forget that "Pedagogy is always related to power" (Giroux, 1992, p. 15). I share with Spiegel (2011) the belief that instructors can have "immense power . . . in disrupting these heteronormative spaces" in ways that recognize and affirm LGBTQIA students (p. 22).

We also have the terrible power to further marginalize these students through our neglect. Instructors must remember that "people who make gender trouble—LGBT people, those who are gender nonconforming—these people take profound risks simply by coming to school" (Blackburn, 2006, p. 264). We owe LGBTQIA students a willingness to educate ourselves in order to effectively educate them. The best educators do what is necessary to meet the students where they are, which requires knowing who they are and some of what they face and being committed to meeting their needs. Agid and Rand (2011) insist that educators committed to equality in the classroom must "use our bodies to project and experiment with possibilities, and to challenge the ways in which, perhaps, our bodies are read against the meanings we would prefer or though relationships of power that malign some bodies—along lines of race, nation, gender, sexuality, gender presentation, class signs, etc.—in favor of others" (p. 8). To respond with cultural competence to LGBTQIA students, instructors must build trust with LGBTQIA students through acknowledgment, affirmation, and inclusion to ensure their classroom are places of centralization rather than marginalization.

Questions for Instructor Reflection

How do I let LGBTQIA students know that I know they are here?

Do I talk as if LGBTQIA persons exist?

Do I use inclusive language?

Do I respond in ways that show I am aware of the impact of their gender and/or sexual identity in their educational experience?

How do I respond to homophobic or heterosexist incidents in the classroom?

Do our instructional materials make evident the contributions of LGBTQIA individuals and fairly illustrate their experiences?

Does our syllabus contain a clear, specific nondiscrimination policy—not just the university's but our own policy for classroom participation?

When I mention campus resources, do I include the LGBTQIA center? Have I visited it?

Suggestions for Further Reading and Action

Download The Safe Zone Project 2-Hour Curriculum. Visit http://thesafezoneproject.com/about/what-is-safe-zone/#. Safe Zone offers LGBTQ awareness workshops. You may download educational materials and/or sign up for an online training on their website. If your college or university offers Safe Zone training, attend in person. Display Safe Zone signs in your office or hallway to let LGBTQIA students know your institutional space is safe for and supportive of them.

Read *Sexuality: A Very Short Introduction* by Veronique Mottier (2008). This slim volume from Oxford University Press offers a brief but adequate primer on the concepts highlighted in this article.

Read "Gender Pronouns" from Lesbian, Gay, Bisexual, Transgender Resource Center at the University of Milwaukee (2017). Visit https://uwm.edu/lgbtrc/support/gender-pronouns/. This is a brief guide to gender neutral and gender nonconforming pronouns.

Watch the video "Pronouns" from Cut's "One Word" project. Visit https://youtu.be/Nn1TC7VEpf4.

Take a Sexuality Implicit Association Test (IAT) from Project Implicit. Implicit association tests measure attitudes and beliefs of which we may be unaware or unwilling to disclose. Visit https://implicit.harvard.edu/implicit/takeatest.html and reflect upon the preferences revealed by your result.

Download the Equality Literacy 101 Glossary from Straight for Equality for definitions of key terms relating to issues of gender and sexual identity diversity. Visit https://bolt.straightforequality.org/files/Come%20Out%20as%20a%20Straight%20Ally/equality-literacy-101-s4e-.pdf.

Visit "Inclusion and Respect: GLSEN Resources for Educators" and browse the offerings for instructors. Though GLSEN targets K-12 educational environments, many of their online Educator Guides are applicable to college classrooms. Visit https://www.glsen.org/educate/resources.

Read "Suggested Best Practices for Supporting Trans Students" by The Consortium of Higher Education LGBT Resource Professionals Trans Policy Working Group (2014). Visit https://lgbtcampus.memberclicks.net/assets/trans%20student%20inclusion%20.pdf.

Read "Recommendation for Supporting Trans and Queer Students of Color" by The Consortium of Higher Education LGBT Resource Professionals (2016). Visit https://lgbtcampus.memberclicks.net/assets/tqsoc%20support%202016.pdf.

Read "Compulsory Heterosexuality and Lesbian Existence" by Adrienne Rich in her book *Blood, Bread and Poetry: Selected Prose 1979-1985*. (1994). W. W. Norton & Company.

Visit "Ask Me: What LGBT Students Want Their Professors to Know" and read the article by Julia Schmalz (2015) and watch the corresponding video. Visit http://www.chronicle.com/article/Ask-Me-What-LGBTQ-Students/232797.

Read "130+ Examples of Cisgender Privilege in All Areas of Life for You to Reflect On and Address" by Sam Dylan Finch

(2016) for *Everyday Feminism.* Visit http://everydayfeminism.com/2016/02/130-examples-cis-privilege/.

References

Agid, S. and Rand, E. (2011). Beyond the special guest—Teaching 'trans' now. *The Radical Teacher,* 92, 5-9.

Blackburn, M. V. (2006). Risky, generous, gender work. *Research in the Teaching of English, 40*(3), 262–271. *JSTOR,* www.jstor.org/stable/40171679.

Blackburn, M. V. and Smith, J. M. (2010). Moving beyond the inclusion of LGBT-themed literature in English language arts classrooms: Interrogating heteronormativity and exploring intersectionality. *Journal of Adolescent & Adult Literacy, 53*(8), 625-634.

Britzman, D. (1998). Is there a queer pedagogy? Or, stop reading straight. *Curriculum: Toward New Identities.* Ed. William F. Pinar. New York: Routledge.

Connolly, M. (2000). Issues for lesbian, gay and bisexual students in traditional college classrooms. In V.A. Wall, & N.J. Evans (Eds.), *Toward Acceptance: Sexual orientation issues on campus* (pp. 109-130). Lanham, MD: University Press of America.

Consortium of Higher Education LGBT Resource Professionals. (2016). Recommendations for supporting trans and queer students of color. Retrieved from https://lgbtcampus.memberclicks.net/assets/tqsoc%20support%202016.pdf.

Consortium of Higher Education LGBT Resource Professionals Trans Policy Working Group. (2014). Suggested best practices for supporting trans students. Retrieved from https://lgbtcampus.memberclicks.net/assets/trans%20student%20inclusion%20.pdf.

Cut. (2015). "Pronouns. Trans. One word." *Youtube.* Retrieved from https://youtu.be/Nn1TC7VEpf4.

Finch, S. D. (2016). 130+ examples of cisgender privilege in all areas of life for you to reflect on and address. *Everyday Feminism.* Retrieved from http://everydayfeminism.com/2016/02/130-examples-cis-privilege/.

EEOC. (2012). Macy v. Holder. No. 0120120821, 2012 WL 1435995. Retrieved from https://www.eeoc.gov/decisions/0120120821%20Macy%20v%20DOJ%20ATF.txt.

Free & Equal: United Nations for LGBT Equality. (2015). Free & equal: Intersex fact sheet. Retrieved from https://unfe.org/system/unfe-65-Intersex_Factsheet_ENGLISH.pdf.

Giroux, H. A. (1992). *Border crossing: Cultural workers and the politics of education.* New York: Routledge.

Glenn v. Brumby, No. 10-14833 ; 10-15015. (2011). Retrieved from http://www.lambdalegal.org/sites/default/files/glenn_ga_20111206_decision-us-court-of-appeals.pdf.

GLSEN. (2017). Inclusion and respect: GLSEN resources for educators. Retrieved from https://www.glsen.org/educate/resources.

GLSEN. (2016). 2015 National school climate survey executive summary. Retrieved from https://www.glsen.org/article/2015-national-school-climate-survey.

Johnson III, R. G. and Rivera, M. A. (2015). Intersectionality, stereotypes of African American men, and redressing bias in the Public Affairs classroom. *Journal of Public Affairs Education, 21*(4), 511-522.

Holloway v. Arthur Anderson and Company. 566 F.2d 659. (1977). Retrieved From https://scholar.google.com/scholar_case? case=3216558323572540298.

Johnston, S. (1995). Not for queers only: Pedagogy and postmodernism. *NWSA Journal 7*(1), Sexual Orientation, 109-122.Lesbian, Gay, Bisexual, Transgender Resource Center at the University of Milwaukee. (2017). Gender pronouns. Retrieved from https://uwm.edu/lgbtrc/support/gender-pronouns/.

Majied, K. F. (2010). The impact of sexual orientation and gender expression bias on African American students. *The Journal of Negro Education, 79*(2), 151–165. *JSTOR*, www.jstor.org/stable/20798333.

Meyer, E. J. (2012). From here to queer: Mapping sexualities in education. *Counterpoints, 367*, Sexualities in Education: A Reader, 8-17.

Mottier, V. (2008). *Sexuality: A Very Short Introduction*. Oxford: Oxford UP.

Mufioz-Plaza, C., Quinn, S. C, & Rounds, K. A. (2002). Lesbian, gay, bisexual and transgender students: Perceived social support in the high school environment. *The High School Journal, 85*, 52-63.

Office of the Federal Register. (2016). Nondiscrimination in health and activities: A rule by the Health and Human Services Department on 5/18/2016. Retrieved from https://www.federalregister.gov/documents/2016/05/18/2016-11458/nondiscrimination-in-health-programs-and-activities.

Oncale v. Sundowner Offshore Services, No. 96—568. (1998). Retrieved from https://www.law.cornell.edu/supct/html/96568.ZO.html.

Price Waterhouse v. Hopkins, 490 U.S. 228 (1989). Retrieved from https://supreme.justia.com/cases/federal/us/490/228/case.html.

Project Implicit. (2017). Sexuality IAT. Retrieved from https://implicit.harvard.edu/implicit/Study?tid=-1.

Reece-Miller, P. C. (2010). Chapter 7: An elephant in the classroom: LGBTQ students and the silent minority. *Counterpoints, 356*, 67–76. *JSTOR*, www.jstor.org/stable/42980600.

Rich, A. (1994). Compulsory heterosexuality and lesbian existence. *Blood, Bread and Poetry: Selected Prose 1979-1985.* New York: W. W. Norton & Company.

Safe Zone Project. (2017). 2-Hour curriculum. Retrieved from http://thesafezoneproject.com/about/what-is-safe-zone/#.

Schmalz, J. (3 Sep. 2015). Ask me: What LGBT students want their professors to know. *The Chronicle of Higher Education.* Retrieved from http://www.chronicle.com/article/Ask-Me-What-LGBTQ-Students/232797.

Shlasko, G. D. (2005). Queer (v.) Pedagogy. *Equity & Excellence in Education 38*(2), 123-134.

Spiegel, M. (2011). The Personal as productive? Sexual embodiment and identity in the Women's Studies classroom. *Counterpoints, 397,* Queer Girls in Class: Lesbian Teachers and Students Tell their Classroom Stories, 21-26. Smith v. City of Salem, Ohio, No. 03-3399. (2004). Retrieved from http://caselaw.findlaw.com/us-6th-circuit/1380020.html.

Straight for Equality. (2017). Equality literacy 101 glossary. *Straight for Equality.* Retrieved from https://bolt.straightforequality.org/files/Come%20Out%20as%20a%20Straight%20Ally/ equality-literacy-101-s4e-.pdf.

U.S. Department of Education Office of Civil Rights. (2017). Dear Colleague. Retrieved from https://www2.ed.gov/about/offices/list/ocr/letters/colleague-201702-title-ix.docx.

Winans, A. E. (2006). Queering pedagogy in the English classroom: Engaging with the places where thinking stops. *Pedagogy: Critical Approaches to Teaching Literature, Language, Composition, and Culture, 6*(1), 103—122.

About the Authors

Catherine Burke

Catherine Burke is a doctoral student in clinical psychology at Spalding University. She has a Native American ancestry and have been frustrated by Western teaching styles throughout her educational career. Catherine is an active member of Spalding's multicultural professional society and devotes her practicum experiences to serving diverse populations. Additionally, she is focusing her dissertation on understanding the psychology of Native Americans.

Michael Daniel & Mackenzie Hoffman

Michael Daniel and Mackenzie Hoffman are currently doctoral students at Spalding University with an emphasis in pediatric psychology. Both authors have been involved with the treatment of students ranging from elementary to college age and have, on many occasions, advocated for their students in the classroom. Research for both of their dissertations involved cognition and learning, with Mackenzie focusing on the effects of stress on critical thinking and Michael examining online learning and learner-centered teaching.

Timothy Forde

Timothy Forde is the Vice Provost for Diversity and Chief Diversity Officer at Eastern Kentucky University (EKU). He is also a faculty member in the School of Education. Dr. Forde received his PhD from Vanderbilt University. He also has a MPH from the University of Alabama at Birmingham. He received his bachelors from Oakwood University in Huntsville, AL. Dr. Forde has approximately 20 years of experience in the areas of diversity, cultural competency and inclusive excellence. In his spare time, he enjoys racquetball, playing the piano and cycling.

Virginia S. Frazier

Mom, wife, and farmer are a sampling of roles Virginia S. Frazier, Psy.D. ("Ginny") juggles alongside her career as the Director of a university-based community mental health center in Louisville, KY. Ginny's involvement with political activism, social justice, and community service began as a teenager (25 years ago) and still permeates throughout her practice and teaching of psychology today. Her dream? To ensure those who need high quality mental health care receive it. Outside of her office, Ginny loves to travel with her wife and 3 children; or spend time on their horse farms in Kentucky and Florida.

Natalie A. Gibson

Natalie Gibson is the System Director for Cultural Diversity with the Kentucky Community and Technical College System. She is a doctoral candidate in Morgan State University's Community College Leadership Development Program. Natalie earned a Master of Public Administration and a Bachelor's degree from the University of Kentucky. Under Natalie's leadership, KCTCS developed its first strategic diversity plan, *Beyond the Numbers,* and received the Charles Kennedy Equity Award from the Association of Community College Trustees in 2011. In 2017, Natalie received the Giving Back Diversity Leadership Award from *INSIGHT into Diversity* magazine. In her downtime, Natalie enjoys travelling with her family, reading and listening to music.

Truman Harris

Truman Harris is a doctoral student specializing in child and adult clinical psychology at Spalding University. He has extensive experience working with marginalized populations with psychological trauma and behavioral disturbances. Truman's work with the refugee and immigrant population and at-risk children and adolescents of color is the focus of his research interests. His dissertation focuses on the institutional barriers that often hinder people of marginalized backgrounds from gaining access to educational, societal, legal, and economic resources.

Carson Haynes

Carson Haynes is a doctoral student at Spalding University specializing in Child, Adolescent, family Psychology. She has two years of direct clinical experience working with both young adults and children in community and private settings in Louisville, KY. She is also extremely interested in topics of race, LGBTQ+, and violence. She has experience working with trauma survivors and is passionate about educating people about issues surrounding trauma and its impact on daily life. Her dissertation is focused on LGBT+ adolescents.

Kaitlyn Hoitomt

Kaitlyn Hoitomt is a doctoral student at Spalding University specializing in Child, Adolescent, family and Health Psychology. She has three years of direct clinical experience working with both adults and children in public, private, and hospital facilities in Louisville, KY. Her additional interests include topics on multiculturalism, LGBTQ+, sexual health, trauma, and grief/dying. Kaitlyn's interest and experience with trauma informed care comes from her extensive experience of working in nationally recognized residential treatment homes for children and hospitals for mental health for the past four years.

Jimmy Joseph

Jimmy is a Haitian-American male born and raised in West Palm Beach, FL. Despite being surrounded by wealth, he spent a majority of his life living the shadow cast by the skyscrapers of the rich. Alongside other Haitian families, Jimmy was surrounded by Jamaicans, Trinidadians, Cubans, Guatemalans, etc. and exposed to a cocktail of culture outside of the westernized majority. These experiences led Jimmy on a path of multicultural exploration. He continues to search for the common threads among cultures of people from various backgrounds.

Steven Kniffley

Steven Kniffley is an Assistant Professor at Wright State University in the School of Professional Psychology. He is also a board certified licensed child psychologist. Dr. Kniffley's area of expertise is research and clinical work with Black males. Specifically, his work focuses on understanding and developing culturally appropriate interventions for Black male psychopathology as well as barriers to academic success for this population. As an educational consultant, Dr. Kniffley has worked internationally with students and school administrators in South Africa and India. He currently serves as a consultant to the Dayton Public School Office of Males of Color.

Meena Kumar & Nisha Kumar

Meena Kumar is a doctoral student specializing in child clinical psychology at Spalding University. She has extensive experience working directly with children, adolescents, and families in school and community settings. Within her experience, she has worked primarily with culturally and racially diverse children and families exposed to trauma. Her dissertation is focused on refugee children's experience of school bullying. Co-author Nisha Kumar is a doctoral student specializing in adult clinical psychology at Pacific University. She has intensive experience working directly with diverse students in college counseling centers. Both Meena and Nisha's shared background in school settings allows for a unique perspective in identifying culturally-appropriate educational practices for students. Additionally, through their education they have experience with navigating the academic culture as quiet, introverted students and seek to increase awareness and understanding regarding introverted students in the classroom.

RoShunna Lea

RoShunna Lea, who began her doctoral degree at the Forest Institute of Professional Psychology, currently attends Spalding University where she is preparing to be a clinical neuropsychologist. Prior to her doctoral studies, RoShunna completed her Master's degree at the Chicago School of Professional Psychology in Washington, DC, where she provided clinical services to minority populations in the public charter schools and Howard University. Through her clinical work and her personal experiences as an African-American navigating the varying dynamics of each graduate program she attended, RoShunna developed unique insight into the cultural issues affecting minority students in academic settings.

Adriana Peña

Adriana Peña is a doctoral student at Spalding University with numerous years of experience related to multicultural topics and engaging with diverse populations through academia, clinical work, and community outreach. Her expertise and interest in multicultural topics began when she mentored gang-affiliated Latino youth in Baltimore. For the last few years, she has focused more on promoting emotional well-being among refugees and immigrants, and advocating for marginalized groups. Currently her research and academic work focuses on promoting racial harmony, evaluating the impact of race-based trauma, and increasing critical consciousness.

Tara Tuttle

Tara M. Tuttle teaches Women's and Gender Studies at Eastern Kentucky University in Richmond, KY Her research examines the effects of religious belief on expressions of female sexuality in contemporary American popular culture and the ways in which members of contested groups use scriptural rhetoric to challenge oppressive practices.

DeDe Wohlfarth

DeDe Wohlfarth received her doctorate in clinical psychology from Spalding University in 1998. She completed her doctoral internship at University of Nebraska Consortium at Boys and Girls Town. Dr. Wohlfarth is a full professor at Spalding University in Louisville, KY, and the Director of the Child, Adolescent and Family Emphasis Area. She recently co-authored a book, *Case*

Studies in Child and Adolescent Psychopathology (Waveland Press, 2017), which shares multicultural, contextual, and complex case studies in a problem-based learning format. Dr. Wohlfarth has more than 30 years of experience working with traumatized children with severe emotional and behavioral problems. Her philosophy of treatment and education is: 1) To look at what is right in others instead of just what is wrong; 2) To use evidence-based methods in her practice; and, 3) To deliver culturally responsive services that celebrate the marvelous diversity of people.

www.ingramcontent.com/pod-product-compliance
Lightning Source LLC
Chambersburg PA
CBHW052101230426
43662CB00036B/1723